D0071738

COMPULSORY PREGNANCY
The War Against American Women

John M. Swomley

HUMANIST PRESS

Amherst, New York

Published in cooperation with Americans for Religious Liberty, P.O. Box 6656, Silver Spring, MD 20916; (301) 598-2447.

Printed and bound in the United States of America.

ISBN: 0-931779-12-X

Cover photo: Erik Alsgaard, *Christian Social Action.*

TABLE OF CONTENTS

PREFACE

Women have been allowed to vote in the United States for less than a century. Although they make up over half of the U.S. population, they are grossly underrepresented in Congress and other lawmaking bodies, in many professions, in the upper ranks of business and industry, and in the leadership of the more conservative religious traditions. The situation for women is even worse in much of the rest of the world.

For many centuries women's social roles were largely restricted to *Kinder, Küche, und Kirche* -- children, kitchen, and church.

On January 22, 1973, the American judicial system, after a few state legislatures had shown some movement in that direction, recognized in *Roe v. Wade* that the constitutional right to privacy covers a woman's right to decide for herself whether or not to continue a problem pregnancy. While most European countries have varying permissive policies on abortion, choice on abortion is not so much a protected constitutional right as it is a legislatively conferred and regulated privilege. Under *Roe v. Wade* the right to choose is constitutionally protected. Unfortunately, however, the Supreme Court has subsequently permitted Congress and state legislatures to dilute that right somewhat with waiting periods, mandated (and not always neutral) counseling, parental notification, restrictions on availability of publicly-funded reproductive health services for poor women, and assorted restrictions for members of the armed forces and their dependents.

Supporters of women's rights hailed *Roe v. Wade* as a Magna Carta or Declaration of Independence for women.

Defenders of patriarchy deplored the ruling. The leadership of the Roman Catholic Church, uninterested in the views of their members, condemned the ruling on the ostensible ground that embryos and fetuses are persons having a "right to life," an "ensoulment at conception" notion that their tradition did not hold for most of its history. Indeed, the basis for the Vatican's position is the view that nothing should be allowed to interfere with the reproductive purpose of sex, neither contraception nor abortion nor sterilization nor same-sex relations.

Protestant opinion varied and varies quite widely on the propriety of abortion under different circumstances. Mainstream Protestant traditions, generally accepting of women's rights of conscience and supportive of women's ordination, has been fairly favorable to freedom of choice, particularly with regard to the role of government in the decision making process. Mainstream opinion is well represented by the Religious Coalition for Reproductive Choice, which embraces much of the Protestant spectrum, four of the five major divisions of American Judaism, Catholics for a Free Choice, Unitarian Universalists, and humanists.

As the 1970s wore on the more fundamentalist Christian traditions tended to fall into the anti-choice camp, ostensibly for biblical reasons (though the Bible does not condemn abortion, but does provide some support for the traditional Christian and Jewish view that personhood begins at birth), but more likely related to sentiment favorable to patriarchy and male dominance.

The right of every woman to choose freely if and when to become a mother, to decide whether or not to continue a problem pregnancy, it seems to me, is found in the democratic ideal of the moral equality of all persons, male and female. It is rooted in the constitutional right to privacy and might even be said to be reinforced by the Thirteenth Amendment prohibition against "involuntary servitude." And while *Roe v. Wade* was based on the constitutional right to privacy, the right to choose should be seen as protected by the First Amendment guarantee of "free exercise" of religion. Further, legislation that would interfere with freedom of choice would seem to violate the First Amendment ban on laws "respecting an establishment of religion" by having the effect of imposing a particular theological notion of "personhood at conception" or "ensoulment at conception."

* * *

This book is a collection of the insightful and remarkably comprehensive writings of John M. Swomley on the subject previously published in a variety of journals.

John Swomley, whom I have been privileged to know and work with for many years, is eminently qualified to deal with this issue. An ordained United Methodist minister, he holds a doctorate in political science from the University of Colorado. From 1960 to 1984 he was Professor of Christian Ethics at the St. Paul School of Theology in Kansas City, Missouri, and is now Professor Emeritus. He has taught biomedical ethics at the University of Kansas Medical Center. He is president of Americans for Religious Liberty and was a long-time board member and sometime vice-president of the American Civil Liberties Union and chair of its church-state committee. He is a member of the Committee on Civil and Religious Liberty of the National Council of Churches.

He has lectured widely around the U.S. and abroad. Indeed, he has lectured literally in countries from A to Z, from Argentina to Zimbabwe, with the Philippines, Korea, the United Kingdom, Belgium, The Netherlands, India, Japan and others in between.

John is the author of such books as *Liberation Ethics; The Politics of Liberation; Religion, the State, and the Schools; Religious Liberty and the Secular State; Myths About Public School Prayer; Religious Political Parties; Confronting Church and State: Memoirs of an Activist;* and *Confronting Systems of Violence: Memoirs of a Peace Activist.* He is co-author, with Albert J. Menendez and myself, of *The Case Against School Vouchers.*

His articles have appeared in *Christian Social Action, The Christian Century, The Humanist, The National Catholic Reporter, USA Today, The Nation, the St. Louis Journalism Review, The Progressive, Christian Ethics Today, The Churchman/Human Quest,* and other periodicals.

* * *

Supplementing Dr. Swomley's writings in this book are the amicus curiae brief presented to the U.S. Supreme Court in 1989 in the case of *Webster v. Reproductive Health Services,* a brief representing a dozen Nobel laureates and other scientists, and relevant material published by Catholics for a Free Choice and the Religious Coalition for Reproductive Choice.

-- Edd Doerr

Edd Doerr is president of the American Humanist Association and executive director of Americans for Religious Liberty.

INTRODUCTION

Abortion rights was a major domestic problem for many years before the procedure was legalized in the 1973 Supreme Court decision *Roe v. Wade*. Prior to that decision as many as one million illegal abortions took place in the United States each year, and hospitals across the country had to care for women who had either attempted abortions themselves and had serious self-injuries or had sought help from untrained practitioners, with disastrous results.

The Cook County hospital in Chicago prior to *Roe v. Wade* admitted annually about 4,000 women for medical care following illegal abortions. After the Supreme Court decision, abortion became not only legal but one of the safest medical procedures, actually safer than childbirth.

However, the safety of women is increasingly threatened today by attempts by those opposing abortion to put a stop to these legal procedures. Violence against women entering clinics has risen and has spread to include attacks on doctors, clinic personnel and family planning institutions.

Even before *Roe v. Wade* numerous countries in Europe legalized abortion either with restrictions or on request. Among them were Sweden, Denmark, Poland, Finland, the Netherlands, the United Kingdom, and Czechoslovakia. Since 1973 France, Spain, Italy, and Belgium have legalized it.

The Vatican opposed legalization and feared the movement away from its teachings. In 1975 the American Catholic bishops, in easily the most detailed religio-political campaign in American history, organized to oppose legalized abortion. It became an important focus of much official church action, even though the campaign was resisted by many progressive Catholics and simply ignored by a great many more. The bishops also set in motion efforts to make this ecumenical, but succeeded only or chiefly with some right wing fundamentalist Protestant evangelists and churches that have kept women in subordinate positions for doctrinal reasons. The bishops flooded Washington with their followers, including thousands of children from parochial schools.

Women's organizations, the American Civil Liberties Union, and other groups defending women's rights responded. One slogan during a pro-choice march in Washington shouted by marchers was: "Two, four, six, eight, not the church, not the state, women will decide their fate."

The Catholic bishops had considerable success with the Reagan and Bush administrations in changing U.S. family planning assistance overseas and in controlling judicial appointments. They succeeded in modifying *Roe v. Wade* and in banning late-term abortions in many states, but failed to get a constitutional amendment to completely overturn the Supreme Court decision.

Cardinal John O'Connor of New York, the Vatican's chief spokesperson, in an April 3, 1992, speech to the most right wing of Catholic universities, Franciscan University of Steubenville, Ohio, said, "The fact is that attacks on the Catholic Church's stance on abortion, unless they are rebutted effectively, erode church authority in all matters, indeed the authority of God himself." In the April 1, 1992, edition of his newspaper, *Catholic New York*, he wrote:

> Abortion has become the number one challenge for the Church in the United States because . . . if the Church's authority is rejected on such a crucial question as human life . . . then questioning of the Trinity becomes child's play, as does questioning the divinity of Christ or any other church teaching.

This is not an overstatement. Pope John Paul II has made abortion the church's highest priority. Wherever he goes on his world tours, opposition to abortion and contraceptive birth control are among the chief points of his message. He has not only instructed U.S. bishops but intervened in American politics in his *Evangelium Vitae*, a March 1995 encyclical that is an explicit instruction to obedient Catholics in Congress, state legislatures, and even the courts in their official capacity, to oppose existing and proposed laws that would permit abortions. Specifically the Pope said, "In the case of an intrinsically unjust law such as a law permitting abortion . . . it is never licit to obey it or take part in a propaganda campaign in favor of such a law or vote for it."

The various organizations that favor freedom of conscience with regard to abortion and contraception have been active but have not been able to match the disciplined organization or huge financial resources available to the bishops and right-wing Catholic and Protestant organizations responsive to their direction.

The strategies of the choice campaign, revelations about its sponsors, and an analysis of these strategies and the case for maintaining legal abortion, are the basis or subject of the articles in this book, which are reprinted from a variety of sources. There is inevitably some overlap in them even though they deal with specific developments as they occurred.

As the author of these articles I find it necessary to expose the arguments and strategy of the Vatican and the bishops. However, I hasten to point out that I have worked closely with various progressive groups and individuals in the Catholic Church on peace and justice issues as well as in defending

Catholic women in their right to freedom of choice on abortion. The Catholic Church is a large and great church, and most of its members do not view abortion as the most important theological or political aspect of their membership. They see war, poverty, disease, racism and liberation from other forms of oppression, as well as the myriad problems of daily life, as their major concerns. They work for a peaceful world, for an environment free from damage by overpopulation and corporate exploitation, and for the right of women to make their own decisions about when and how to have children. Catholic women use contraception at the same rate as Protestant and Jewish women. Their abortion rate is slightly higher. And their husbands stand with them.

So the abortion controversy is one led by the all-male patriarchy of the Catholic and Protestant right wing. And women's and various other organizations who support women's right to reproductive freedom are on the defense in the controversy.

I became seriously concerned about the rights of women to reproductive freedom because of the women in my life, beginning with my mother's concern. I was also influenced by my concern for separation of church and state. No church or its leaders should impose its theology or authority by law in a secular (i.e., religiously neutral) state or on the people of their own and other religions or no religion.

I have also been influenced by Catholic women whom I have defended in legislative hearings and in other settings. And I believe with every fiber of my being that minorities of religion, race, and sexual orientation should not be intimidated by religious patriarchy.

My vision of freedom has been expanded over the years not only by women, but by my service or leadership roles in Americans for Religious Liberty, the American Civil Liberties Union, the United Methodist Church, the Religious Liberty Committee of the National Council of Churches, the Missouri Family Health Council, the University of Kansas Medical Center's bioethics program, and other organizations.

Finally, I would like to express my thanks to Matt and Terri Stark of Minneapolis, and the Jackson Social Welfare Committee of First Unitarian Universalist Church in Ann Arbor, Michigan, for grants that made publication of this book possible, to Edd Doerr for his editorial assistance, and to all of the courageous women and men who have labored long for freedom of conscience, civil liberties, and equal rights for women.

John M. Swomley
Kansas City, Missouri
October 1999

ABORTION AND PUBLIC POLICY

My purpose in this article is to demonstrate that abortion per se is not morally wrong, but should be left to private decision and medical judgment. The alternative to private decision making and medical judgment is compulsory pregnancy if the government adopts laws prohibiting or restricting abortion prior to the third trimester when there is evidence of viability. In stating the case for the right of a woman to terminate an unwanted pregnancy, it is essential first to define *abortion* and examine the claim that a human being exists at conception, responding to the question, "When does human life begin?" Therefore, I shall examine the claims made on behalf of fetal life as over against the rights of existing persons, public policy with respect to women, the issue of covert violence against women inherent in compulsory pregnancy, questions of conscience, and finally, some specific legislative proposals.

The anti-abortion movement in the United States began with the Pro-Life Pastoral of the Catholic bishops in 1975.[1] It is therefore appropriate to accept the official church definition that any intentional termination of a pregnancy after the moment of conception is an abortion.[2]

It is misleading, however, to speak of "a moment of conception" when sperm meets egg following sexual intercourse. Conception is not complete or viable until the fertilized egg is implanted in the uterus, which generally occurs about ten days to two weeks after ovulation.[3] Up to fifty percent of fertilized eggs do not implant, and in those cases it is not possible to speak of conception.[4] Except in cases of *in vitro* fertilization, it is impossible to know that fertilization has taken place until implantation occurs.[5]

Charles Gardner, who did his doctoral research on the genetic control of brain development at the University of Michigan Medical School's Department of Anatomy and Cell Biology, writes, "The 'biological' argument that a human being is created at fertilization . . . comes as a surprise to most embryologists . . . for it contradicts all that they have learned in the past few decades."[6] Gardner notes that

> in humans when two sibling embryos combine into one . . . the resultant person may be completely normal. If the two original embryos were determined to become particular individuals, such a thing could not happen. The embryos would recognize themselves to

Reprinted with permission from The St. Louis University Public Law Review, *Vol. III, No. One (1993).*

be different . . . and would not unite. But here the cells seem unaware of any distinction between themselves. . . . The only explanation is that the individual is not fixed or determined at this early stage.[7]

Gardner also writes, "The fertilized egg is clearly not a prepackaged human being. . . . Our genes give us a propensity for certain characteristics, but it is the enactment of the complex process of development that gives us our individual characteristics. So how can an embryo be a human being?"[8] He further states, "The information required to make an eye or a finger does not exist in the fertilized egg. It exists in the positions and interactions of cells and molecules that will be formed only at a later time."[9]

Such research and discoveries lead to the conclusion that a developmental process taking about nine months produces a human being. Therefore the idea that a human exists at conception is a theological statement rather than a medical or scientific fact. Gardner concludes that "[f]ertilization, the injection of sperm DNA in the egg, is just one of the many small steps toward full human potential. It seems arbitrary to invest this biological event with any special moral significance. . . . It would be a great tragedy if, in ignorance of the process that is the embryo, state legislators pass laws restricting individual freedom of choice and press them upon the people. The embryo is not a child. It is not a baby. It is not yet a human being."[10]

The use of the term "baby" or "child" or "human being" to describe an embryo or fetus is a propaganda device known as prolepsis, which *Webster's Dictionary* defines as "an anticipating, especially the describing an event as if it had already happened," when in fact it may be months away or may never happen. For example, no one who eats a fertilized egg says he has just eaten a chicken, nor is the crushing of an acorn the destruction of an oak tree.

Since the driving forces to make abortion a public policy issue are a few Christian groups, including the Catholic bishops and followers of Protestant fundamentalist leaders,[11] it is worth citing biblical answers to the key question in the abortion controversy: "When does human life begin?" The Bible's clear answer is that human life begins at birth with breathing. In Genesis 2:7, God "breathed into his nostrils the breath of life and man became a living being" (in some translations, "a living soul.") The Hebrew word for a human being or living person is *nephesh*, the word for breathing. "Nephesh" occurs hundreds of times in the bible as the identifying factor in human life. This is consistent with modern medical science, as a group of 167 distinguished scientists and physicians told the Supreme Court in 1988, "the most important determinant of viability is lung development," and "viability has not advanced to a point significantly earlier than 24 weeks of gestation" because critical organs, "particularly the lungs and kidneys, do not mature before that time."[12]

In the Christian scriptures, the Incarnation, or the "Word made Flesh"[13] was celebrated at Jesus' birth, not at a speculative time of conception. The biblical tradition is followed today by counting age from the date of birth rather than from conception, a date people do not know or seek to estimate. The state issues no conception certificates, only birth certificates. It issues no death certificates for fertilized eggs that do not implant or for miscarriages.

The 167 scientists stated,

> Fetal brain development is obviously a long and incremental process. Brain cells in the neocortex, the portion of the brain in which the processes we call thought, emotion and consciousness occur, must be sufficiently developed to permit this kind of neurological activity to take place. At about 28 weeks of gestation, brain development is marked by the sudden emergence of dendritic spines in the neocortex. Dendritic spines are essential components in the brain's cellular circuitry."[14]

The brain is the crucial element in human life. Michael V.L. Bennett, chair of the Department of Neuroscience, Albert Einstein College of Medicine, wrote that "personhood goes with the brain and does not reside within the recipient body. . . . There is none, not heart, kidney, lung or spleen, that we cannot transplant, do without, or replace artificially. The brain is the essence of our existence."[15] It cannot be transplanted.

Fifty-one percent of all abortions in the United States occur before the eighth week of pregnancy; more than ninety-one percent by the twelfth week, in the first trimester; and more than ninety-nine percent by twenty weeks,[16] which is about four weeks before the time of viability when ten to fifteen percent of fetuses can be saved by intensive care.[17] This means that there is no brain or neocortex and hence no pain.

Up to fifty percent of fertilized eggs do not implant.[18] Of those that do, between twenty percent and fifty percent miscarry.[19] Of all implantations, only about ten percent are successful pregnancies.[20] If there is no objection to the prevention of implantation as a method of abortion, on the assumption that this is the taking of life, then nature or God is the greatest killer, because there are more spontaneous preventions of implantation than those performed medically. In other words, there is no natural or divine evidence that every conception should eventuate either in implantation or in birth. This is consistent with our previous assertion that a fetus, as well as a fertilized egg, is a potential rather than an actual human being.

Public policy in the United States is and should be guided by secular considerations rather than theological claims that are inconsistent with scientific and medical research. The Constitution of the United States is a secular document which gives no authority to government to legislate theological assertions or to prefer the theological doctrines of one or several religious groups over others.[21] A large number of religious groups in the United States--Jewish, Christian, and Humanist--do not accept a "moment of conception" theology or view a fetus as a person or human being.[22]

Public policy must defend the rights of existing living persons as over against claims made on behalf of fetal life. There are generally three claims made for fetal life other than the claim of human being or personhood, which has been discussed above.[23] The first claim is that society should protect innocent human life that is unable to protect itself. The term "innocent," originally used by various popes, refers to fetal life which has committed no sin.[24] Yet the Roman Catholic Church has proclaimed only one person, Mary, the Mother of Jesus, as having an immaculate conception and hence free from original sin.[25] In any event, public policy cannot be founded on theological claims to innocence.

There is another meaning of "innocence" which comes from two Latin words, *in* (not) and *nocere* (to harm), and therefore means "not harmful or dangerous."[26] However, it is precisely the fact that some pregnant women (and their physicians) view the fetus as harmful or threatening to their health or welfare and hence leads them to consider abortion.[27]

A second claim made on behalf of fetal life is that there is a right to life that takes precedence over the life or health or welfare of the pregnant woman. In discussing this claim we must distinguish between a virtue, that is, doing something that may be considered desirable, and a right. If I am walking along the bank of a river or lake and someone who cannot swim falls or jumps in, we could argue that I ought also to jump in, to rescue the drowning person, even if my own life is at stake. But the person who jumps or falls in cannot claim that I must jump in because he/she has a right to life. The mere fact that I *ought* to rescue another does not give that person a right against me.[28]

The common law rule is that we have no duty to save the life of another person, unless we voluntarily undertake such an obligation as a lifeguard does in contracting to save lives at a swimming pool.[29] Neither is there a biblical mandate that each of us is morally required to risk our lives to save the life of another. Jesus treated as highly exceptional and an evidence of great love the act of a person who "lay down his life for his friends."[30]

No woman should be required to give up her life or health or family security to save the life of a fetus that is threatening her well-being. At the very least she is entitled to self-defense.[31] On the other hand, many women are willing to sacrifice their health and future in order to have one or more children. The community that respects the autonomy of women must respect equally their freedom of choice.

A third claim for fetal life is that no fetus should be denied the right to be born and make the most out of life. Let us take the case of *in vitro* fertilization, a process whereby male sperm fertilizes a female egg in a test tube or dish. Can it be argued that such a fertilized egg has all the rights of a living person? Does it have the right to be implanted in a woman's uterus, without which there could be no expectation of childbirth? *In vitro* fertilization is forbidden by the Vatican statement, "Instruction on Respect for Human Life in its Origin and on the Dignity of Procreation."[32] Fr. Donald McCarthy of the Pope John XXIII Medical, Moral and Educational Center in St. Louis has called for the endowment of civil rights to every fertilized egg, including the right not to be created at all except as a consequence of "personal, self-giving and conjugal love."[33] Here two fictional legalisms conflict: a human being exists at "conception," but that human being has a right not to be implanted. Who makes that decision? Certainly not the fertilized egg. Why is this any different from saying that an unwanted fetus has a right not to be born?

There are at least two rights which must be considered in answering the question whether the fact of sexual intercourse implies the right of the fetus to be born. The first is the right of a community, such as the state, to ensure its survival. A community following a nuclear war or a plague that had virtually destroyed all human life might expect a pregnant woman to bear the child. By the same logic, any community, whether a family or a state, which already had more people than it could furnish with food and water, could restrict the number of childbirths.[34] There are already children dying by the thousands in some parts of the world because of too little water and food and no foreseeable future prospect of change.[35] What is the inherent right of thousands of fetuses to be born if they will jeopardize the existence of those already born?

The shortage of water in the southwestern United States, particularly in California, is a familiar and serious problem.[36] Predictions for the Mideast are that Jordan's natural water supply will be exhausted by 2010. "Jordan then will be totally dependent on rain water and will revert to desert. Its ruin will destabilize the entire region. . . . All Middle East economies must be restructured away from agriculture because of a lack of water."[37]

The second right that takes precedence over claims that a fetus has a right to be born is individual rights of existing human beings. The moral foundation of democracy is individual liberty: the freedom to choose what to believe, what to say, what to read, and what to do, free from government interference. The exception to this is that such freedom must not interfere with the freedom or rights of others.

The government has no moral right to compel its citizens to do anything unless the failure to do so would endanger the community or the security of the state, such as fighting a forest fire that threatened a town or accepting vaccination against a rapidly spreading contagious disease. However, there would be no moral right to compel only certain classes of citizens--for instance, women, racial minorities, or those over sixty-five to engage in such activity.

The government, for example, even by majority vote of the legislature, has no moral right to tell a married couple that they must bear children or never bear children. There is no moral right to tell a woman, married or unmarried, that she must become or remain pregnant against her will. Compulsory pregnancy is a form of slavery, just as compulsory labor, referred to in the Constitution as involuntary servitude,[38] is contrary to human freedom. Compulsory pregnancy may aggravate a woman's serious health problems, drastically affect her work and income, and hence endanger the stability of her family and the well-being of existing children.

The fact that a woman has had sexual intercourse with her spouse or partner is not a contract for pregnancy. The Roman Catholic hierarchy doctrine that every sexual act must be open to procreation assumes that a sexual relation is an implied contract for pregnancy.[39] If that, for Catholics, is enforceable by church action, it certainly should not be applied to non-Catholics who do not accept that teaching, and therefore it should not directly or indirectly become government law.

Sometimes overzealous "right to life" advocates compare Dred Scott and the Supreme Court case[40] bearing his name with a similar lack of rights according to fetal life.[41] This is a mistaken analogy. A fetus has never been a person in Anglo-Saxon law.[42] Persons exist only at birth. The issue in the *Dred Scott* decision was whether a slave recognized as property in slaveholding states could become a citizen of the United States if a free state conferred its citizenship upon the slave.[43] The Court said not. However, this judgment did not apply to all blacks, for the Court said, "And if persons of the African race are citizens of a State, and of the United States, they would be entitled to all of these privileges and immunities in every State and the State could not restrict them."[44]

The similarity or parallel between the *Dred Scott* decision and the Court's abortion decision is this: The abolitionists who wanted to end human slavery fought against the *Dred Scott* decision. Those who want women to be enslaved by laws requiring childbirth if a woman is impregnated by rape, incest, failure of contraception, etc., are fighting against the Supreme Court decision legalizing abortion. The abolitionists fought for the freedom and right of self-determination of black slaves. The pro-choice movement fights for the right of women legally to determine their own destiny and to control their bodies. *Dred Scott* symbolized the inequality of black slaves with free white and free black men. The problem today is that "right to life" political and religious leaders want to take millions of women and make them as class not only unequal to men but subordinate to the fetuses they carry in their wombs.

This is well illustrated by an August 19, 1988, *New York Times* editorial, which said of the 1988 Republican Party platform that when "given a choice between saving the fetus or the mother, the mother must die."[45] Marjorie Bell Chambers, platform committee member from New Mexico, moved to amend the proposed platform language "that the unborn child has a fundamental right to life which cannot be infringed" by dropping the last four words."[46] She argued that in the conflict between saving the fetus or the life of woman, the phrase "cannot be infringed" meant "that men and fetuses have a right to life at all times, but women lose that right when they become pregnant."[47]

Those opposing Ms. Chambers' amendment unequivocally argued that a fetus took precedence over a woman's life.[48] The platform committee defeated her amendment fifty-five to thirty-three with eleven abstentions.[49]

The political problem involved in all public policy discussion of abortion is the status of women in our society. Only in this century have women had the right to vote.[50] Only recently have women had access to contraceptives and family planning.[51] Women have to struggle against church and state to gain equality with men. Papal doctrine is quite specific about the role of women in that "a woman is by nature fitted for home work . . . not suited for certain occupations."[52] Pope John Paul II said that paid work outside the home is the abandonment of the role of motherhood, which includes "taking care of her children" and "is wrong from the point of view of the good of society and of the family when it contradicts or hinders these primary goals of the mission of a mother."[53]

The present pope fails to realize that many families including actual children could not exist in modern society without both parents working outside the home, to say nothing of women who head single-parent families. These factors may lead a woman who cannot otherwise hold her family together, sometimes with the additional care of an invalid husband or parent, to choose an abortion. The root of the problem is not in modern economics, but in stereotyping of women and in assigning different treatment to them than to men.

Women, whose lives and freedom have been largely at the mercy of men for centuries, must make or be involved in decisions that affect their lives, their futures, their families. To refuse on principle to permit a woman to consider her life or welfare when it seems threatened by pregnancy is to say that only men are the recipients of political freedom and responsibility. It is also to say that the primacy of the right to bodily life of the fetus places all other considerations, including the health, worth, and dignity of women, on a lower level.

The pro-life position is really a pro-fetus position and the pro-choice position is really pro-woman. Those who take the pro-fetus position define the woman in relation to the fetus. They assert the rights of the fetus over the right of a woman to be a moral agent or decision maker with respect to her life, health, and family security.[54]

What right does a woman have to an abortion? One answer is that the rights of living persons take precedence over any rights of potential persons, just as immediate or present needs take precedence over probable future or potential needs. The question can also be stated as: What right does anyone have to impose mandatory pregnancy on a woman? The ethical question is not whether abortion can be justified, but whether we focus on an embryo or fetus as the object of value or whether we focus on the woman as a moral agent who must have freedom of choice.

In addition to the fact that, like Dred Scott, women have not received equal treatment with men, women experience violence in our macho or male-dominated society. The overt type of violence includes such acts as rape, spousal abuse, and sexual harassment.[55] The covert type, frequently hidden behind the myth that motherhood and care of children define a woman's role, has been institutionalized in religious, economic, and political systems and enforced by legislation and custom.[56] One illustration of this covert violence against women is inherent in what is, in fact, compulsory pregnancy. A woman made pregnant through incest or rape (and rape can take place inside as well as outside of marriage) has no choice; others have controlled her body and well-being. Another no-choice situation involves women compelled to remain pregnant because of a failed contraceptive. During the three-year period 1979-1982, "there were 1.61 million contraceptive failures per year" and "the typical woman would experience 0.81 failures during her lifetime."[57]

Today almost half of the women seeking abortions do so because of a failed contraceptive.[58] The failure rate of barrier methods is in the ten to eighteen percent range; of birth control pills, one to four percent; of Norplant, .04 percent; and of natural family planning, twenty to thirty-five percent.[59]

There is violence also in the idea embodied in some legislation that a poor woman may have a publicly funded abortion only if the pregnancy endangers her life.[60] This means that any damage to a woman's health short of death is "acceptable" violence; suffering brought by exacerbation of existing health problems such as diabetes or heart disease and the shortening of her life thereby are "acceptable" violence. The imperiling of a woman's mental health is also a type of violence.

When it is assumed that a woman, by the fact of intercourse, "asks for" pregnancy, there is an element of puritanical punishment or revenge in the idea that once pregnant she must be compelled to remain so. The man, who is equally responsible for the pregnancy, is not similarly "punished."

In effect, this would mean that a woman who does not want a child, but who becomes pregnant from rape, incest, failed contraception, or ignorance about her reproductive processes, must serve as a surrogate mother without pay for the benefit of another person or couple, since the major proposed alternative to abortion is adoption. Forcing women to bear children they do not want and cannot support or care for, and then go through the trauma of giving them away is a form of violence.

The New York Times on July 27, 1984, reported that there were more than 50,000 legally available children in the United States who had not been adopted.[61] An official of the National Adoption Exchange said there was no problem "when it came to healthy white babies . . . [but] [w]e have children who have emotional, physical or developmental difficulties . . . and a large number are black or Hispanic."[62] The unwanted fetus whom the right-to-life advocates say should not be aborted is often unwanted by parents seeking an adoption and must therefore be cared for by the state.[63]

What about fetal deformity? Legislators considering banning of abortions do not generally consider this an exception, however severe.[64] Yet such a birth, besides being a serious psychological blow to a woman, might involve full-time childcare for her for twenty or more years.

Violence occurs in the requirement of parental notification by teenagers before they can get an abortion. Most teenagers who seek an abortion do consult at least one parent, but some feel unable to do so for various reasons, such as fear of being beaten or killed, exiled from the family, or psychologically rejected.[65] At least one teenager, to my knowledge, committed suicide in the mistaken notion that she could not face her parents. In most of these cases there is a different standard for the female, who has been made pregnant by a male who walks away and bears no legal responsibility. The violence is borne solely by the teenage girl or her family.

Incest is one of the reasons for teenagers not consulting parents about pregnancy. The National Center for Child Abuse and Neglect states that there are at least 100,000 cases of sexual abuse each year.[66] Some estimates are as high as 250,000.[67] Between twelve and twenty-four percent of incest victims become pregnant.[68] Exposing abuse within one's family bring both trauma and reprisals. So the insistence on laws requiring parental consent is a form of violence against young women.

A proposal that has some influence with those who seek nonviolent solutions is the "consistent life ethic," linking opposition to abortion, the death penalty, and war.[69] At first glance this seems a logical unity against violence. It is, however, not consistent in respecting the lives of women faced with a dangerous pregnancy. Like other absolute rules, there is no recognition of a conflict of life with life. Therefore, embryonic life is given priority over the life of the existing woman. Moreover, this idea, which originated with a member of the Catholic hierarchy, Cardinal Bernardin, treats women who have abortions differently from those who participate in war or in the death penalty.[70] Women who have abortions are automatically excommunicated; judges, juries, and executioners who inflict the death penalty, and CIA agents or military personnel who kill again and again are not excommunicated or held up to scorn.[71] Thus, the "consistent life ethic" is chiefly directed against pregnant women, and is a form of covert violence.

The complexities of the abortion controversy have kept many religious groups and conscientious individuals from condemning abortion.[72] This is true even in churches with dogmatic positions against abortion. One peace-minded group that has historically opposed killing is the Society of Friends (Quakers).[73] The General Committee of the Friends Committee on National Legislation in 1975 recognized the dilemma in the abortion controversy in adopting the following statement:

> Members of the Religious Society of Friends (Quakers) have a long tradition and witness in opposition to killing of human beings, whether in war or capital punishment or personal violence. On the basis of this tradition, some Friends believe that abortion is always wrong.
>
> Friends also have a tradition of respect for the individual and a belief that all persons should be free to follow their own consciences and the leading of the Spirit. On this basis, some Friends believe that the problem of whether or not to have an abortion, at least in the early months of pregnancy, is one primarily of the pregnant woman herself, and that is an unwarranted denial of her moral freedom to forbid her to do so.
>
> We do not advocate abortion. We recognize there are those who regard abortion as immoral while others do not. Since these disagreements exist in the country in general as well as within the Society of Friends, neither view should be imposed by law upon those who hold the other.

Recognizing that differences among Friends exist, nevertheless we find general unity in opposing the effort . . . to say that abortion shall be illegal.[74]

On the other hand, some religious groups, notably the Catholic Church, have sought and received public funds for their extensive system of hospitals.[75] So long as abortion is legal, physicians in those hospitals ought not to deny a woman an abortion. Yet here conscience also should prevail. No physician conscientiously opposed to performing an abortion should be forced to do so. By the same token, women whose conscience tells them to have an abortion should not be forbidden by church or state.

Episcopal Bishop George Leslie Cadigan stated the case for conscience:

It is at once the glory and the burden of each of us that we are called upon to make such difficult personal decisions according to our conscience. When we deny that liberty to any one of our number, we give away a part of our own birthright. When, more specifically, we condemn a woman for making an independent judgment according to her own conscience, relating to her reproductive life, we denigrate her personhood.

The "rightness" or "wrongness" of abortion as the solution of a problem pregnancy is not the critical issue here. The issue is the larger ethical one: can any one of us stand in the role of judge for the personal decisions of others? What robes shall we wear? Greater than the debatable immorality of terminating an undesired pregnancy is the immorality of refusing a woman access to medical help when she has determined that she needs it.[76]

A study by a Canadian psychiatrist, Dr. Paul K.B. Dagg, in the May 1991 *American Journal of Psychiatry* provides objective confirmation of the consequences if abortion is denied.[77] Children born after their mothers were denied abortions suffer profound social and psychological problems well into adulthood, and women who are denied abortions experience similar problems.[78] Dr. Dagg reviewed much of the literature available in English, including studies conducted overseas. He indicated in general terms that open abortion (chosen freely by women) is received as a positive experience by most women. He stated, "Longer term studies, over months and years show . . . the majority of women express positive reactions to the abortion, and only a small minority express any degree of regrets."[79] His study also found that "legal abortion of an unwanted pregnancy in the first trimester does not pose a psychological hazard for women."[80] But when abortion is denied, he reported among children of unwanted pregnancy "a more insecure childhood, more psychiatric care, more childhood delinquency" and other problems.[81]

Before outlining specific public policy proposals it is necessary to ask the question I asked students in my biomedical ethics classes: "If there were no unwanted pregnancies, would there be a significant abortion problem?" They generally concluded that the real problem is unwanted pregnancies. However, the anti-abortion movement will not deal with unwanted pregnancies by advocating sex education in the public schools or contraceptive birth control or economic measures to minimize abortions for working mothers or those with low income. They simply want to pass laws against abortion.

If the United States had declared yellow fever to be illegal and had ignored the mosquitoes that were causing it, the United States would have made the same mistake as the "right-to-lifers": neglecting the cause and concentrating on the result. In short, the anti-abortion movement concentrates on the result instead of the cause and is an effort to punish women and physicians rather than to deal with the problem.

Public policy in the United States should begin with and include the following:

1) There should be mandatory sex education in the public schools, taught by competent and specially-trained teachers so that pregnancy from reproductive ignorance may be avoided.

2) The United States government should encourage and if necessary subsidize the development of safe and effective contraceptives so as to prevent unwanted pregnancies. This should include the availability of effective contraceptives produced in other countries, such as RU-486.[82]

3) Since women whose family income was less than $11,000 were almost four times as likely to have an abortion as women with family incomes of more than $25,000,[83] there should be a guaranteed annual income for families below the poverty level as well as guaranteed health care, including free contraceptives.

4) There should be no legislation criminalizing or restricting abortion before the third trimester or the viability of the fetus. Thereafter states may regulate abortions except when the life or health of the woman is threatened or the fetus is diagnosed as having a serious disease or lack of an organ or brain that threatens its future.[84]

5) If churches or states are insistent that women with deformed or retarded fetuses should not have an abortion, they should provide institutions for the care of deformed or retarded children whose parents cannot or will not provide for them.

6) Conscience as an integral part of religious liberty should be protected for health care workers who do not want to participate in providing abortion

or contraceptives. Likewise, the consciences of women who seek or have an abortion should be respected. This means that physicians, clinics, and women visiting them should be free from intimidation and harassment by groups like Operation Rescue. Likewise, such anti-abortion groups should have the right of peaceful picketing on public property so long as unrestrained access to clinics by those who want to use them is permitted.

7) Finally, public policy must conform to constitutional guarantees of separation of church and state. Theological definitions of "human being" and "personhood" or religious rules about sex, the status of women, or reproduction ought not to be written into law unless scientifically validated and required for the health or safety of the state or its citizens.

Public policy in the United States is and should be guided by secular rather than theological claims that are inconsistent with scientific and medical research. The Constitution of the United States is a secular document which gives no authority to government to legislate theological assertions or to prefer the theological doctrines of one or several religious groups over others. A large number of religious groups in the United States--Jewish, Christian, and Humanist--do not accept a "moment of conception" theology or view a fetus as a person or human being.

In fact, the Fourteenth Amendment to the Constitution accepts the physical evidence of birth in its statement, "All persons born or naturalized in the United States . . . are citizens of the United States."[85] The time and date of conception are at least speculative. Public policy and law cannot be based on an event that may or may not eventuate in childbirth.

Endnotes

[1] *Pastoral Letters of the United States Catholic Bishops* (High J. Nolan ed., 1983).

[2] See *1993 Catholic Almanac* 295 (1993).

[3] See *Dorland's Illustrated Medical Dictionary* 369 (27th ed. 1988).

[4] Henri Leridon, *Human Fertility*, 79-81 (1977).

[5] Laboratory tests are available to detect pregnancy "as early as 7 to 9 days after ovulation, very soon after implantation occurs." Robert A. Hatcher, M.D. et al., *Contraceptive Technology 1990-1992*, at 433 (1992).

[6] Charles Gardner, "Is an Embryo a Person?", *Nation*, Nov. 13, 1989, at 557.

[7] *Id.*

[8] *Id.*

[9] *Id.*

[10] *Id.*

[11] See Darrell Holland, "Abortion Foes Hold Vigil as Rights Groups Hail Orders Clinton Signed," *Plain Dealer*, Jan. 23, 1993, at 10A.

[12] Amicus Curiae Brief of 167 Distinguished Scientists and Physicians, including 11 Nobel Laureates, at 10-12. *William Webster v. Reproductive Health Services*, 492 U.S. 490 (1989) (No. 88-605) (hereinafter *Amicus Brief*).

[13.] John 1:14.

[14.] *Amicus Brief, supra* note 12, at 14.

[15.] Michael V.L. Bennett, "Personhood from a Neuroscientific Perspective," in *Abortion Rights and Fetal Personhood*, 77 (Edd Doerr & James W. Prescott eds., 1990).

[16.] *Abortion Factbook, Readings, Trends, and State and Local Data to 1988* 65 (S.K. Henshaw & J. Van Vort eds., 1992).

[17.] *Amicus Brief, supra* note 12, at 12-13.

[18.] Dr. Henry Morgentaler, *Abortion and Contraception* 23 (1982).

[19.] *Id.* (quoting Porrier et al., *Embryologie Humaine* (1973)).

[20.] *Id.*

[21.] U.S. Constitution, amendment I.

[22.] Bennett, *supra* note 15, at xviii-xix.

[23.] Ruth Marcus, "Administration Renews Call for Abortion Ruling," *Washington Post*, April 7, 1992, at A22.

[24.] See *43 Acta Apostalicae Sedis* 857 (1951); see Loraine Boettner, *Roman Catholicism* 158 (1962); see Pius XII, *Moral Questions Affecting Married Life* 26 (1951).

[25.] Kenneth L. Woodward & Rachel Mark, "What Mary Means Now," *Newsweek,* Jan. 1, 1979, at 52.

[26.] *Webster's Seventh New Collegiate Dictionary* 436 (1970).

[27.] Aubrey Milunsky & Leonard H. Glantz, "Abortion Legislation: Implications for Medicine," *248 JAMA*, 833-834 (1982).

[28.] *Restatement (Second) of Torts* §314 (1965).

[29.] *Id.* at §324.

[30.] John 15:13.

[31.] John F. Derek, *Human Life* 43 (1972).

[32.] Kevin Doran, *What Is a Person? The Concept and the Implications for Ethics* 144-52 (1989).

[33.] Quoted in *Kansas City Star.*

[34.] See, e.g., Karl Zinsmeister, "Let a Dozen Flowers Bloom," *Heritage Foundation Policy Review* 30 (Fall 1989).

[35.] See, e.g., Ford Fessenden, "Diseases Adding to Death Rate," *Newsday,* December 11, 1992, at 39.

[36.] Ed Mendel & Steve La Rue, "State raises water-delivery estimate to 55% but environmental restrictions will bar return to pre-drought levels now or ever, officials say," *San Diego Union Tribune*, Feb. 16, 1993, at A3.

[37.] Elias Salameh, founder and former director of University of Jordan's Water Research and Study Center, in "Rains Wash Away Some of Mideast's Conservation Urgency," *Washington Post*, May 14, 1992, at A16.

[38.] U.S. Constitution, amendment XIII.

[39.] See, e.g., D'Arcy Jenish, "The Wrath of Rome," *Maclean's,* February 15, 1993, at 50.

[40.] *Dred Scott v. Sandford*, 60 U.S. 393 (1856).

[41.] See Stephen Chapman, "Abortion, Slavery and the Boundaries of the Human Race," *Chicago Tribune*, July 29, 1993, at 19.

[42.] James Tunstead Burtchaell, *Rachel Weeping: The Case Against Abortion* 239 (1984), and Connie Paige, *The Right to Life* 47 (1983).

[43.] 60 U.S. at 422.

[44.] *Id.* at 423.

[45.] "George Bush's Gender Gap," *New York Times*, August 19, 1988, at A26.

[46.] "Republican Platform Puts Fetus Before Mother," *New York Times,* September 27, 1988, at A34.

[47.] *Id.*

[48.] *Id.*

[49.] *Id.*

[50.] U.S. Constitution, amendment XIX.

[51.] *Griswold v. Connecticut*, 381 U.S. 479 (1965); *Eisenstadt v. Baird*, 405 U.S. 438 (1972).

[52.] *The Great Encyclical Letters of Pope Leo XIII* 235 (1900); *The Papal Encyclicals 1958-1981* 318 (1981).

[53.] Pope John Paul II, *Laborem Exercens*, September 14, 1981, at para. 91.

[54.] See, e.g., "Republican Platform Puts Fetus Before Mother," *New York Times*, September 27, 1988, at A34.

[55.] See, e.g., L.A. Kauffman, "Sexual Harassment: How Political is the Personal?, *Nation*, March 26, 1988.

[56.] See Renita Weems, "My Other Me," *Essence*, October 1993, at 69.

[57.] Hatcher, Stewart, et al., *Contraceptive Technology 1990-1992* 136 (1992).

[58.] Henshaw & VanVont, *supra* note 16, at 78.

[59.] Id.; see also, J. Trussel et al., "Contraceptive Failures in the U.S.: An Update, *Studies in Family Planning* 21 (1) (1990).

[60.] Many states, such as Georgia, Mississippi and Missouri, fund abortions only if life is endangered.

[61.] Sheila Rule, "In Search of Parents for the 50,000 'Other' Children," *New York Times*, July 24, 1984, at B1.

[62.] *Id.*

[63.] *Id.*

[64.] Pennsylvania Senate Bill, enacted as Act 64 on November 17, 1984, makes no exception for fetal deformity. "Who Decides? A State-By-State Review of Abortion Rights," *The NARAL Foundation* 134 (1991). Thirty-five states do not permit public funding for abortions for fetal deformity. Id. at 184.

[65.] "Our Daughter's Decisions," *The Alan Guttmacher Institute* 22 (1992); "Parental Notice Laws--Their Catastrophic Impact on Teenagers' Right to Abortion," *ACLU Reproductive Freedom Project* 5-6 (1986); "Teenagers, Abortion, and Government Intrusion Laws," *Planned Parenthood Education of America, Inc.* 2 (1992).

[66.] Ellen Weber, "Incest-Sexual Abuse Begins at Home," *Ms.*, April 1977, at 64-65.

[67.] *Id.*

[68.] S. Kirson Weinberg, "Incest," in *Problems of Sex Behavior* 178-79 (Edward Sagarin & Donal E.J. MacNamara eds. 1968).

[69.] See, e.g., Kurt Chandler, "Abortion Talks Are Calm Eye of the Storm: Some Activists Looking for Common Ground," *Star Tribune*, August 2, 1993, at 1B.

[70.] See Kenneth A. Briggs, "Bishops' Debate," *New York Times*, October 26, 1984, at A24.

[71.] Andrew J. Cuschieri, O.F.M., *Introductory Readings in Canon Law* 251 (1988).

[72.] See Mark Weston, "Where the World's Major Religions Disagree," *Washington Post*, January 23, 1990, at Z12.

[73.] Paul C. French, *We Won't Murder* 43-45 (1988).

[74.] Friends Committee on National Legislation, Statement to Congressional Committees in Opposition to Constitutional Amendment Preventing Abortion.

[75.] See Gary Born, "Church and State and the Family Life Act: U.S. Has History of Supporting Churches' Work," *Manhattan Lawyer*, May 3-9, 1988, at 32; *Bradfield v. Roberts*, 20 S. Ct. 121 (1899).

[76.] See, e.g., John M. Swomley, "Abortion and the Law," *Church & State*, Vol. 29, No. 10 (November 1976).

[77.] Paul K.B. Dagg, "The Psychological Sequelae of Therapeutic Abortion -- Denied and Completed," *148 American Journal of Psychiatry* 578 (1991).

[78.] *Id.* at 583.

[79.] *Id.* at 583.

[80.] *Id.* at 579.

[81.] *Id.* at 583.

[82.] See, e.g., Kathleen Day, "French Maker of Abortion Pill Shows Reluctance to Enter the U.S. Market," *Washington Post,* January 23, 1993, at A9.

[83.] Henshaw & VanVont, *supra* note 16, at 75.

[84.] When I testified before a Kansas Senate Committee in March, 1992, a young Catholic woman testified following my statement. Between sobs she said she had already given birth to two children and never dreamed she would seek an abortion. When the fetus she was carrying in her third trimester was diagnosed as having only about one-fourth of a heart and would die a painful death, she got no support from her priest and could not get a late abortion in Virginia. When she arrived in Wichita to get a late abortion, fanatical Operation Rescue demonstrators surrounded the bus in which she and others approached the clinic. Demonstrators shouting "Murderer" and "Baby killer" imprisoned her on that bus for 48 hours.

[85.] U.S. Constitution, amendment XIV.

ONE NATION UNDER GOD . . .

A massive political campaign is underway in an effort to achieve religious and political control of crucial American policies and institutions, an effort which the popular press and television have virtually ignored. It was inspired by the Vatican and has been carried out over a period of years under the supervision of the National Council of Catholic Bishops. The bishops have created the impression that they speak for 59 million Catholics, which makes them a formidable political force, able to influence or intimidate presidents and other public officials.

For example, they had an important and close relationship with President George Bush. Within a month after Bush took office he included all five of the U.S. cardinals in meetings at the White House and, thereafter, Cardinals Bernard Law of Boston and John O'Connor of New York spent overnights at the White House as guests of the president.

Doug Wead, a special assistant to the president, was quoted in the December 29, 1989, *National Catholic Reporter* as saying that Bush "has been more sensitive and accessible to the needs of the Catholic Church than any president I know of in American history. . . . We want the Church to feel loved and wanted, and want them to have input." That relationship and input was maintained through the cardinals. Wead also boasted that "this administration has appointed more Catholic cabinet officers than any other in American history." There were, however, a number in the Reagan administration, as well.

The bishops organized their political campaign in 1975 and outlined it in an internal pastoral letter for Catholic officials and organizations. It is an ambitious campaign aimed at controlling judicial appointments, Congress, and other national and state political offices. In his book *Catholic Bishops in American Politics*, Catholic writer Timothy A. Byrnes calls the bishops' plan the "most focused and aggressive political leadership" ever exerted by the American Catholic hierarchy.

This political campaign, which has been organized around the issues of abortion and certain forms of birth control, has wider implications. The ability to control political and judicial offices on one doctrinal issue can and will be used on other matters, such as aid to parochial schools to the neglect of public schools and use of welfare legislation to provide funds for the charitable activities of churches, among others.

Reprinted by permission from The Humanist, *May/June 1998.*

In their plans, the bishops list twenty major Catholic organizations -- such as the Knights of Columbus, the Catholic Press Association, the Catholic Physicians' Guild, and the Catholic Lawyers Association -- then begin to "explain political strategy and discuss how each group may participate." This involves getting "the National Organizations . . . to inventory their internal political capabilities systematically by means of their own government relations" and to "establish a communications structure from Washington to the national office of each organization to activate support for the political program."

A primary focus of the bishops' campaign is judicial appointment, so as to reverse Supreme Court decisions that legalize abortion. "Efforts should be made to reverse the decision, to restrain lower courts from interpreting and applying [Supreme Court decisions] more aggressively and more absolutely than the Supreme Court," the plans dictate. The bishops also "urge appointment of judges" who can be counted on to oppose abortion.

They have already been successful in that only anti-abortion judges were appointed during the Reagan and Bush years -- not one single pro-choice judge was named to the bench. Today, over 70 percent of our federal judges are basically anti-abortion, as are at least four Supreme Court justices.

In order to influence the appointment of judges, it was necessary for the bishops to influence or control other branches of government. So a threefold strategy was "directed toward the legislative, judicial, and administrative areas." This meant that "all Church sponsored or identified Catholic national, regional, diocesan and parochial organizations and agencies [must] pursue the three-fold effort."

When Ronald Reagan was elected president, a major effort was made to influence him, especially at the point of foreign policy. The only popular press coverage of this was a feature by Carl Bernstein in *Time* magazine on February 24, 1992. Bernstein reported that "the key administrative players were all devout Roman Catholics": CIA Chief William Casey; National Security Advisors Richard Allen and William Clark; Secretary of State Alexander Haig; Ambassador at Large Vernon Walters; and Reagan's first ambassador to the Vatican, William Wilson.

Time also reported that, "in response to concerns of the Vatican, the Reagan Administration agreed to alter its foreign aid program to comply with the church's teachings on birth control. . . . 'American policy was changed as a result of the Vatican's not agreeing with our policy,' Wilson explained. 'American aid programs around the world did not meet the criteria the Vatican had for family planning." The Agency for International Development "sent various people from [the Department of] State to Rome,' said Wilson, 'and I'd accompany them to meet the president of the Pontifical Council for the Family, and in long discussions they finally got the message.'" The Vatican was directly involved through Pio Laghi, its apostolic delegate to Washington, D.C., with the Catholic members of Reagan's team, according to the *Time* article.

According to Dr. R.T. Ravenholt, presidential candidate Jimmy Carter made a deal on August 31, 1976, with a group of Catholic bishops headed by Archbishop Joseph Bernardin in which the bishops, by agreeing not to endorse Carter's opponent, Gerald Ford, received major concessions in terms of Catholic political appointees who dismembered and crippled the State Department's family planning programs. Ravenholt, who was serving as director of AID's global population program, was removed.

The legislative branch of government, according to the bishops' plan, requires a more complex organization to cover every congressional district. Immediately after the campaign plan was formulated in 1975, the bishops began to "establish in each diocese a Pro-Life Committee to coordinate groups and activities within the diocese with respect to federal legislative structures." This committee "will act through the diocesan Pro-Life Director, who is appointed by the Bishop to direct pro-life efforts in the diocese." The committee also included a congressional district representative to "develop core groups with close relationships to each Senator or Representative [and organize a] grass roots effort in every Congressional district." Whenever there is a "House Recess Schedule," the plan "makes the task of visiting the representative in his/her district both imperative and achievable."

At the congressional level, the bishops already have a staunch supporter of the Vatican in Henry Hyde. As chair of the House Judiciary Committee, he has taken the initiative in promoting an anti-abortion amendment to the U.S. Constitution. It is Hyde who is currently promoting the Istook amendment, which would make government funds available for religious organizations. [The Istook Amendment was defeated in the House of Representatives on June 4, 1998.] In 1996, Hyde also chaired the Republican Party's Platform Committee, which has consistently given fetal life rights superior to those of pregnant women.

In each state, there is also a state coordinating committee to work on state politicians and legislators -- the bishops have neglected nothing. They ask Catholics to "elect members of their own group, or active sympathizers, to specific posts in all local party organizations." In other words, the bishops have established an organization in each parish, diocese, state, and on other levels in an effort to take control of American politics, knowing full well that most Americans do not vote and are often not informed of religious groups' determination to achieve their political goals.

The funding for this political effort comes from the bishops' own budget, which in 1993 provided $1.8 million -- more than three times the next largest budgeted item. However, other major sources of funding include the Knights of Columbus and wealthy Catholic donors, such as the owner of Domino's Pizza and the Coors beer family.

Another aspect of the bishops' plan is their ecumenical effort to organize Protestant evangelists and churches as "front" groups, so as to avoid anti-Catholic criticism or recognition that there is a Catholic campaign to control politics. At this level, they have been highly successful in bringing into their campaign the Southern Baptist Convention, the Mormons, and numerous other groups led by Protestant evangelists, including Pat Robertson, Jerry Falwell, and D. James Kennedy, and lay leaders, including Missouri Senator John Ashcroft of the Assemblies of God.

Although the bishops have an extensive publicity network, they are quite content to let these Protestant groups get major attention in the public press, so long as they serve Vatican interests. The combination of these groups, together with the Catholic pro-life organizations, are loosely known as the religious right wing. These individuals and groups are represented formally or informally by such organizations as the Council on National Policy, the Christian Coalition, and organizations founded by Catholic right-wing leader Paul Weyrich: the Heritage Foundation and the Free Congress Foundation. They oppose separation of church and state, reproductive freedom for women, family planning, and equal rights for gays and lesbians and, in general, favor aid to parochial schools or home schooling over adequately financed public schools. On this latter issue, although a majority of Catholic children, especially lower-income Catholics, attend public schools, no cardinal or bishop is an outspoken advocate or defender of public education. It is not a Vatican priority or concern and, on all of the above issues, the Catholic and Protestant right wingers are united.

It is ironic and perhaps significant that the Christian Coalition is being investigated on the extent to which their contributions are illegal, since they claim to be a wholly religious organization not involved in politics. Meanwhile, the Catholic church and Catholic organizations which are clearly involved in political activity have not been so investigated.

There is a very large group of progressive Catholics who are pro-choice and favor birth control, equal rights for women, religious liberty, and public education; in general, they support candidates with such views. However, they are not organized politically so as to espouse or give comfort to progressive politicians. Nevertheless, they provided the margin of votes for the Clinton-Gore reelection ticket in the twelve most heavily Catholic states, even though the bishops strongly attacked Clinton for his veto of a late-term abortion bill and in quiet ways supported the Republican ticket. This demonstrates that the bishops do not speak for all Catholics and that politicians who are not intimidated by the bishops' campaign can often win against those who do yield to the bishops' political efforts.

Still, the threat to America posed by the Catholic bishops and their Protestant allies is very great. At the very least, their efforts could lead to some form of shadow theocratic government, such as in southern Ireland where the bishops collectively are known as the "purple parliament."

What is required to counter this is a clear exposé of the Catholic bishops' campaign and their collusion with the Protestant right wing which they assisted in organizing (see the March/April 1996 *Humanist*), coupled with a strong counter-offensive in defense of church-state separation. It should also be obvious that organizations like the American Civil Liberties Union, which depend upon an independent judiciary and judicial defense of the Bill of Rights, cannot be effective if the separation of church and state is eroded and congressional majorities are dominated by the religious right wing.

New strategies, new organizations of progressive voters, and more grass-roots education must become the order of the day. Until that happens, it is essential to alert everyone about the Catholic campaign for America and its Protestant allies.

THE HUMAN LIFE AMENDMENT: CONTRARY TO RELIGIOUS LIBERTY

The anti-abortion movement has for many years sought language for a constitutional amendment that would ban all abortions and at the same time most forms of contraception. Three far-right Republican senators, Robert C. Smith of New Hampshire, a Roman Catholic, and Jesse Helms of North Carolina and John Ashcroft of Missouri, both fundamentalist Protestants, have introduced such an amendment and additional legislation with similar wording.

The proposed amendment states:

> The right to life is the paramount and most fundamental right of a person. With respect to the right to life guaranteed to persons by the Fifth and Fourteenth Articles of Amendment to the Constitution, the word "person" applies to all human beings irrespective of age, health, function or condition of dependency, including their unborn offspring at every stage of their biological development, including fertilization.
>
> No unborn child shall be deprived of life by any person: Provided, however, that nothing in this article shall prohibit a law allowing justification to be shown for only those medical procedures required to prevent the death of either the pregnant woman or her unborn offspring as long as such a law requires every reasonable effort to be made to preserve the lives of both of them.

A constitutional amendment requires a two-thirds vote in both houses of Congress and ratification by three-fourths of the states.

In case an amendment fails or seems likely to fail, the same senators propose back-up legislation to accomplish the same purpose. That legislation would use the same language "to exercise the power of Congress under Section 5 of the Fourteenth Amendment not to deprive persons of life without due process of law" by redefining the word person to apply to "unborn offspring at every stage of their biological development, including fertilization." This legislation could be adopted by Congress and would not require ratification by the states.

Published by the Religious Coalition for Reproductive Choice, 1999. Reprinted by permission.

In each proposal the word person would be redefined so that the fertilized egg would begin personhood. Since only some religious organizations or churches use this definition, the adoption of such language would mark the end of a secular Constitution and make the Constitution the captive of religions that consider fetal life beginning with fertilization more important than the woman in whose womb the conceptus is implanted.

At fertilization such a "person" would weigh a small fraction of an ounce, have no body, no brain, and no sex, and yet considering the fetus to be a person would affect many laws and practices. For example, how it would affect the constitutional requirement of a census of all persons so as to determine how many representatives to Congress each state elects.

The connection between personhood and birth, which has existed for thousands of years, undoubtedly came from ancient days and includes the biblical understanding that personhood exists only when a child is able to breathe on his or her own, apart from the oxygen delivered through the uterus. The Hebrew word for a human being is *nephesh*, the word for breathing. It is ironic that such Protestant fundamentalists as Jesse Helms and John Ashcroft would repudiate a biblical definition of personhood for one that is anti-biblical.

There is also a practical reason for defining personhood at birth. The moment of birth is known; the moment of fertilization is speculative. Former Supreme Court Justice Tom Clark asserted that "the law deals in reality, not obscurity; in the known rather than the unknown. When sperm meets egg life may eventually form, but quite often it does not. The law does not deal in speculation."

If the proposed changes to the Constitution were adopted, that would occur because of fairly recent papal teaching. For centuries Roman Catholic dogma did not assume that a fertilized egg or an embryo or fetus was a human being or a person. In 1679 Pope Innocent XII or his office said it was "lawful to procure abortion before ensoulment of the fetus . . . It seems probable that the fetus (as long as it is in the uterus) lacks a rational soul and begins first to have one when it is born; and consequently it must be said that no abortion is homicide."

Recent popes, while opposing abortion, have not taken the step to declare the conceptus a person but have acted as if it is by banning all contraceptives used after intercourse to prevent implantation of the fertilized egg in the uterus.

It is misleading to speak of a "moment of conception" when sperm meets egg. Conception is not complete until the fertilized egg is implanted in the uterus, which generally occurs about ten days to two weeks after ovulation. Up to 50 percent of fertilized eggs do not implant, and in those cases it is not possible to speak of conception or the possibility of life. Except in cases of in vitro fertilization, it is impossible to know that fertilization has taken place until implantation occurs.

Therefore this proposed amendment would forbid all forms of contraception that prevent implantation, including the intra-uterine device (IUD) and emergency contraception, often called the "morning-after" pill. Only periodic or total abstinence or barrier contraceptives such as the condom and diaphragm could be recommended, prescribed, or sold.

There is no scientific basis for declaring a fertilized egg a person. Michael V.L. Bennett, chair of the Department of Neuroscience, Albert Einstein College of Medicine, wrote that "personhood goes with the brain and does not reside within the recipient body. . . . There is none, not heart, kidney, lung, or spleen, that we cannot transplant, do without, or replace artificially. The brain is the essence of our existence."

Charles Gardner, an embryologist, makes this more explicit:

> The "biological" argument that a human being is created at fertilization . . . comes as a surprise to most embryologists . . . for it contradicts all that they have learned in the past few decades . . . In humans when two sibling embryos combine into one, the resultant person may be completely normal. If the two original embryos were determined to become particular individuals, such a thing could not happen. The embryos would recognize themselves to be different . . . and would not unite. But here the cells seem unaware of any distinction between themselves . . . the only explanation is that the individual is not fixed or determined at this stage. . .

The information required to make an eye or a finger does not exist in the fertilized egg. It exists in the positions and interactions of cells and molecules that will be formed at a later time.

Dr. Gardner further said,

> The fertilized egg is clearly not a prepackaged human being . . . Our genes give us a propensity for certain characteristics but it is the enactment of the complex process of development that gives us our individual characteristics. So how can an embryo be a human being?

If a person does not exist medically or scientifically before brain development and if many religions do not accept personhood or a human being as existing in a fertilized egg, then this effort to legislate personhood at fertilization is either unwarranted or an attempt to inflict a specific religious assumption on people of other religions or none.

Stated another way, the assumption that a person exists at fertilization is based on acceptance of a genetic theory of the beginning of personal life, instead of a developmental observation that includes obvious stages such as the development of heart, lungs, kidney, liver, and brain and the ability to exist outside the uterus.

The origin of this non-scientific redefinition of personhood is in the U.S. Roman Catholic bishops' "Pro-Life Pastoral plan for Pro-Life Activities," issued in November 1975, which mobilized all official church organizations politically to bring about "passage of a Constitutional Amendment providing protection for the unborn child . . . passage of federal and state laws, and adoption of administrative policies that will restrict the practice of abortion as much as possible."

This was a plan deliberately devised to advocate political actions and had a second strategy: to obscure its Catholic leadership by seeking to involve non-Catholic groups. Accordingly, key lay Catholics were used to persuade TV evangelists Jerry Falwell and Pat Robertson to get involved in politics and to encourage Southern Baptists, Mormons, and various evangelicals and fundamentalists to join the anti-abortion effort. They did join and even accepted the bishops' extended interpretation of abortion to include opposition to many forms of contraception.

As a result of this merging of right-wing Catholic and Protestant political efforts, fundamentalist Protestants, including Senators Helms and Ashcroft, have abandoned the biblical definition of personhood and other biblical principles and accepted papal theological and ethical judgments. Abortion, for example, was practiced in biblical times and is not mentioned in the Bible except as a test for a woman suspected of infidelity.

In effect, the new political definition of personhood was coined in the Vatican and under the lead of the U.S. bishops and accepted by right-wing fundamentalists.

The basis for the proposed Constitutional amendment is a relatively recent papal teaching. Pope Pius XII, on October 29, 1951, said, "Now the child, even the unborn child, is a human being in the same degree and by the same title as its mother . . . So . . . to save the life of the mother is a most noble end, but the direct killing of the (unborn) child as a means to that end is not lawful." This means that it is better for the mother to die than it is to save the life of the mother through a direct abortion.

The proposed Constitutional amendment accepts this papal language--"No unborn child shall be deprived of life by any person"--but admits the possibility that a future law might be adopted "to prevent the death of either the pregnant woman or her unborn offspring so long as such as law requires every reasonable effort to be made to preserve the lives of both of them." In other words, the enactment of any such law might or might not be acceptable to the religious forces behind this amendment. Certainly such a protection for the mother is not within the main requirement of the proposed amendment; it would require another law to ensure it.

This proposed amendment does not mean that the bishops or the Vatican speak for all American Roman Catholics. There is substantial evidence that a large majority of U.S. Catholics use contraception and believe that under some circumstances abortion is acceptable. Catholics for a Free Choice, a Washington, DC-based organization, is an important voice for those Catholics. There is also a Catholic reform movement that believes in freedom of conscience, as do numerous Catholic nuns.

The amendment, however, is intended to have all Catholics follow papal rules despite the fact that Catholic women not only use contraceptives but resort to abortion at least as much as Protestant women. The records of the Chicago Planned Parenthood Association prior to the Supreme Court decision legalizing abortion revealed that, during a 12-month period, 2,000 Roman Catholic women were sent to New York for abortions (where they were then legal). They represented more than 40 percent of the women sent to New York from that area, a higher percentage than Jews or Protestants.

If the proposed amendment signifies that a person exists at conception, does this imply that the various states must issue conception certificates instead of birth certificates? If the Catholic practice of baptizing in utero a dying or dead fetus is acknowledgement that a person has died, does this also imply that state authorities must issue death certificates?

The Vatican's single-minded or obsessive concern to deny women reproductive freedom is evident in the proposal advanced by the bishops and their rightwing Protestant allies. The amendment would put an end to legal abortions and certain forms of contraception. It would not, however, end abortion. As many as an estimated one million illegal abortions took place in the U.S. each year prior to the Supreme Court decision in 1973. No law can prevent women from having abortions if they are determined to end a pregnancy. The attempt to prevent abortions is unenforceable unless individual pregnant women are kept under constant surveillance and their homes subject to unannounced invasion. What the law can do is prevent hospitals and doctors from performing medically safe abortions.

Before Kansas legalized abortion, according to Dr. William Cameron, professor of obstetrics at the Kansas University Medical Center, the medical center always had a ward of 20 to 30 beds with patients with blood poisoning or other serious self-injury. "Now," he said, "we almost never have a case like that." Cook County Hospital in Chicago, before the Supreme Court decision, admitted each year about 4,000 women for medical care following illegal abortions. After the decision, there were fewer than five such cases a month.

Churches have the same rights as others to argue for or against abortion but the American people, irrespective of their position on abortion, would be making a great mistake to permit a church to write its theological views about conception or sex into the Constitution. In fact, it would not necessarily be an evasion of the issue for a politician to be against abortion but also oppose a Constitutional amendment prohibiting abortion. In a secular state, government should adopt laws against abortion only if abortion adversely affects the public health or welfare and not because church leaders regard it as sinful.

The proposed amendment raises many serious questions. Can the law deal with the problem of abortion? As observed earlier, prohibiting abortion would almost certainly lead desperate women into evading the law. Redefining American personhood and citizenship would be a great blow to democracy. Efforts to stabilize population growth and the development of new methods of post-coital contraception would be forbidden. Women needing abortion for health reasons who could afford to go to other countries would do so; poor women would be denied the opportunity. Family values would shift from caring adequately for existing children to providing poorly for each successive birth, and many mothers would be unable to work. Even with help from family, a woman continually pregnant would not be acceptable to most employers.

The proposed "right to (fetal) life" amendment also violates the fundamental principles of a free society. It assumes that a woman has no right to make a decision regarding her health or the welfare of an existing family. The amendment in effect legislates compulsory pregnancy. It also violates the right of the husband or potential father who may be forced to stand by passively watching his wife's or partner's health decline, knowing that he may be the one to bear the burden of raising and supporting the child, together with any children that may already be born. It is, as Catholic ethicist Daniel Callahan observed, "a fundamental principle of a free society that those who will be affected by the actions and decisions of others ought to have a voice in the making of those decisions."

The question of legislating the right to life of a fertilized egg is not simply one of preserving a conceptus or preserving the life of a woman if it is at stake. Callahan referred to "the case of a mother with too many children and too few material, familial, social or psychological resources to care for them" and concluded that "The full human meaning of the act of abortion is preservation of the existing children."

Another serious dimension of the proposed amendment relates to the survival of the human species. Does the concept of "the sanctity of life" refer only to present fetal life, or does it refer to the survival of collective human life or of the species? As population continues to grow, problems of scarce natural or water resources and diminished food supplies could require limiting births. We must also keep in mind that the proposed amendment would outlaw major forms of contraception. An increase in population is virtually certain.

It is obvious that this proposed amendment would give potential human beings a superior right over existing human persons. The amendment is so worded as to give the embryo or fetus the same right to life as that of the woman in whose womb the egg has been fertilized and/or implanted. Thus, if the woman's health is so seriously impaired that she will die after the child is born, that is not to be taken into account. Yet there is a whole range of consequences or values that might be jeopardized if the fetal right to life is the overriding consideration. For example, an in vitro fertilization or the fertilized egg in a dish or test tubes would have the same protection as the women who sought the fertilization. Since the proposed amendment guarantees a right to life, presumably it gives the fertilized egg a right to be implanted in the uterus of a woman, even if she changes her mind about receiving an artificially fertilized egg. A woman who underwent fertility treatment would be forced to bear six or eight or ten potential children because she could not subsequently limit the fertility treatment to only one or two--to whom she could give adequate care.

Dr. Edward Rynearson, a physician at the Mayo Clinic, told a group of Methodist clergy some years ago: "I want you to think of this happening to your 16-year-old daughter. Visualize her as having been kidnapped by a group of men, held prisoner in a cabin for ten days and repeatedly raped. It is later found that she is pregnant. What would you want for your daughter? Never mind the statistics or your moralizing. What would you really want?" Under the proposed amendment, she would have to have the unwanted baby.

Episcopal Bishop George Leslie Cadigan said in 1971:

It is at once the glory and the burden of each of us that we are called upon to make such difficult personal decisions according to our consciences. When we deny that liberty to any one of our number, we give away a part of our own birthright. When, more specifically, we condemn a woman for making an independent judgment according to her own conscience relating to her reproductive life, we denigrate her personhood.

The "rightness" or "wrongness" of abortion as the solution of a problem pregnancy is not the critical issue here. The issue is the larger ethical one: can any one of us stand in the role of judge for the personal decisions of others? What robes shall be wear? Greater than the debatable immorality of terminating an undesired pregnancy is the immorality of refusing a woman access to medical help when she has determined that she needs it.

The response of the anti-abortionists to such ideas as permitting women to follow their consciences is that abortion is murder and the law cannot tolerate murder. Abortion is neither murder nor any other form of homicide, because the victim of a homicide must be a human being who has been born and is alive. Just as the digging up of a sprouting acorn is not the same as the cutting down of an oak tree, so it is incorrect to speak of terminating a pregnancy as murder.

If the ending of fetal life were murder, then it would not have been permitted to save the life of the mother, as it was throughout the United States prior to the Supreme Court decision. Even the Catholic bishops who think of it as murder were not prepared to try women for murder after a self-inflicted abortion. If the planned ending of pregnancy were murder, then a miscarriage due to negligence would be a homicide punishable by law.

Opposition to abortion does not necessarily mean advocacy of a Constitutional amendment prohibiting it. Nor does opposition to such an amendment imply approval of abortion. The basic reason for opposing an amendment that defines personhood as beginning at fertilization is religious liberty. When millions of Jews, Protestants and other Americans, including many Catholics, live by a different sexual and medical ethic than that of the Catholic bishops and fundamentalist Protestants, it is not the business of government to intervene in the private sexual relations of human beings and force them to reproduce contrary to their consciences. Is such a position anti-Catholic or anti-fundamentalist? Not at all. Every church is a better church if it wins the loyalty or obedience of its people instead of relying on the government to enforce church teaching.

THE POPE AND THE PILL

Why does the pope oppose contraceptive birth control, family planning and abortion? Does the Vatican not know that there are many countries where the food supply, arable land and water are not enough to care for present or future populations?

A number of Catholic countries in Latin America have abortion rates two to four times higher than in the United States, yet the Catholic bishops there have not launched a crusade against abortion and birth control, as the bishops have in the United States. Why not? Is it because the laws there conform to papal policy and that is sufficient? The answers to these and other related questions have been almost completely ignored by the religious and secular press.

The birth control story begins with the Second Vatican Council in the early 1960s and the decision of two popes to re-examine the church's position on birth control. Pope John XXIII had intended to begin that re-examination, but he died before he could begin the process. His successor, Pope Paul VI, appointed a Papal Commission on Population and Birth Control.

That commission was two-tiered: (1) a group of 15 cardinals and bishops; (2) a group of 64 lay experts representing a variety of disciplines. A member of the lay commission, Thomas Burch, a professor at Georgetown University in the 1960s, said the pope had asked them to try to find a way to change the church's position on birth control without destroying papal authority.

Commission Voted for Change

After two years of study, the lay commission voted 60 to 4, and the clergy voted 9 to 6, to change the position on birth control, even though it would mean a loss of papal authority, because it was the right thing to do. However, a minority report was submitted to the pope. The co-author of that report was a Polish archbishop, Karol Wojtyla, who later become Pope John Paul II.

A Roman Catholic historian and theologian, August Bernhard Hasler, tells the story in his 1979 book, *How the Pope Became Infallible*. He provided the following quotation from that minority report, which actually was the one accepted. It clearly sets forth the basis or reason for the current Catholic crusade against birth control and family planning:

Reprinted by permission from Christian Social Action, *February 1998.*

If it should be declared that contraception is not evil in itself, then we should have to concede frankly that the Holy Spirit had been on the side of the Protestant churches in 1930 (when the encyclical Casti Connubii was promulgated), and in 1951 (Pius XII's address delivered before the Society of Hematologists in the year the pope died).

It should likewise have to be admitted that for a half a century the Spirit failed to protect Pius XI, Pius XII, and a large part of the Catholic hierarchy from a very serious error. This would mean that the leaders of the Church, acting with extreme imprudence, had condemned thousands of innocent human acts, forbidding, under pain of eternal damnation, a practice which would now be sanctioned. The fact can neither be denied nor ignored that these same acts would now be declared licit on the grounds of principles cited by the Protestants, which popes and bishops have either condemned or at least not approved (page 170).

Dr. Hasler concluded: "Thus it became only too clear that the core of the problem was not the pill, but the authority, continuity, and infallibility of the Church's magisterium."

In conformity with this minority report, Pope Paul VI issued his 1968 encyclical, *Humanae Vitae*, in which he condemned every form of contraceptive birth control. Hasler wrote: "After the promulgation of the encyclical . . . the Church conducted a massive purge of its key personnel wherever it could" (page 283).

In other words, the problems associated with countries that are overpopulated and the political campaign in the United States to deny reproductive freedom to women are all due to the papal decision to protect the authority and "infallibility" of the papacy.

"A Source of Incalculable Harm"

Hans Küng, arguably the world's leading Catholic theologian, wrote: "This teaching [against contraceptive birth control] has laid a heavy burden on the conscience of innumerable people, even in industrially developed countries with declining birth rates. But for the people in many under-developed countries, especially in Latin America, it constitutes a source of incalculable harm, a crime in which the Church has implicated itself" (cited in Stephen Mumford, *The Life and Death of NSSM 200*, page 203).

Confirmation of the Church's fear that papal infallibility would be compromised has occurred in recent years in connection with abortion.

Cardinal John O'Connor, in an April 3, 1992, speech at the Franciscan University of Steubenville, Ohio, said, "The fact is that attacks on the Catholic Church's stance on abortion, unless they are rebutted effectively, erode church authority in all matters, indeed the authority of God himself." He said, according to the April 9 edition of his newspaper, *Catholic New York*:

Abortion has become the number one challenge for the Church in the United States because . . . if the Church's authority is rejected on such a crucial question as human life . . . then questioning of the Trinity becomes child's play, as does questioning the divinity of Christ or any other Church teaching.

Politicians Should Enact Laws

Unfortunately the Vatican is not content with applying its dogma against contraceptive birth control to members of the Roman Catholic Church. Pope John Paul II in his *Instruction on Respect for Human Life in its Origin and on the Dignity of Procreation* has declared that Catholic teaching must become law. The *Instruction* states: "Politicians must commit themselves, through this intervention upon public opinion, to securing the widest possible consensus on such essential points. . . . " They are expected to enact into law "appropriate legal sanctions" for violations of the law.

The Vatican wants to outlaw contraceptive birth control because of its stance that there should be no interference with conception. There are, however, means that function after sexual intercourse to prevent implantation in the uterus, such as the IUD and certain pills. Conception, of course, is not complete until the fertilized egg is implanted in the uterus. Nevertheless, this type of birth control is also to be outlawed, the Vatican says.

These strictures, if enacted into law, would put the majority of the population, which is non-Catholic, along with non-conforming Catholics, into the position of being lawbreakers. Non-Catholics even today are affected if they use Catholic hospitals and compliant physicians, since they are forbidden to provide information about contraceptives or to prescribe or apply them.

The problem with papal infallibility, aside from its requirement that Catholics are expected to accept it without question, is that no human being is free from error. We are all creatures of our culture, our education, and our vested interests. The Pope tries to avoid this criticism by insisting that he is the vicar or spokesman for God or Christ. Yet the very fact that he asserts infallible authority over millions of people who must obey him is a radical departure from the teachings of Jesus, who told his disciples:

You know that those who are supposed to rule over the Gentiles lord it over them, and their great men exercise authority over them. But it shall not be so among you; but whoever would be great among you must be your servant. . . . (Mark 10:42-43).

Both Jesus and the Apostle Paul rejected the legalism inherent in the papacy's infallible rules.

WAR AND THE POPULATION EXPLOSION: SOME ETHICAL IMPLICATIONS

The nature of war has been changing from wars between nations to wars within nations. According to the United Nations, only three of the eighty-two armed conflicts between 1989 and 1992 were between nations. Those within nations were primarily the result of religion or culture or race or ethnic differences, poverty, shortage of arable land, and inequalities caused by overpopulation.

There have been 148 wars in the world since World War II, according to Ruth Sivard, a military analyst. Among these were wars in the Sudan, Somalia, Bosnia, Rwanda, and Ethiopia. Most of these were population wars.

These new wars, characterized as "population wars," can be contrasted with imperialist wars during the period 1500 through the early 20th century, when major powers sought conquest of territory for the exploitation of resources. Spain, France, Britain, Portugal, Holland, Germany and the United States were all involved in such wars. The chief factor in all such conquests was armaments or military and naval superiority over the more poorly armed natives in India, Africa, and the Americas. By the 20th century nations or combinations of nations fought wars so disastrous as to lead them to carve out spheres of influence or alliances to deter war, and conferences to limit armaments and establish rules of warfare. Still World Wars I and II occurred.

Today the United States as the world's "superpower" has established spheres of influence in the Americas; in Europe, through NATO; and in Asia through treaties with Japan, the Philippines, South Korea and others. The U.S. is now in the process of extending its power throughout the Middle East. Within these spheres of influence the U.S. recognizes that hunger, poverty, refugees, migration, shortages of water, and overpopulation are major threats to peace and stability. Or, as in the case of Africa, it tends to ignore grave turmoil and social upheavals where there are fewer political and economic interests at stake.

The Pentagon is aware of this new phase of warfare. In its 1997 Quadrennial Defense Review it justifies its large military establishment in part with these words: "Some governments will lose their ability to maintain public order and provide for the needs of their people, creating the conditions for civil unrest, famine, massive flows of migrants across international

---

Reprinted with permission from Christian Ethics Today, *June 1998.*

borders . . . Uncontrolled flows of migrants will sporadically destabilize regions of the world and threaten American interests and citizens."

The Pentagon's description, together with support evidence to be discussed later, requires a new ethical approach to war in addition to traditional methods of limitation of armaments and other efforts to prevent wars between nations. The new ethical dimension requires serious efforts to reduce population, end degradation of the land and water resources, and reduce poverty worldwide. None of these can be accomplished without fundamental changes in the way women are treated, including their right to reproductive freedom, and the way governments respond to the burgeoning population problem.

The evidence of a planetary population problem includes the cataclysmic increase in the number of economic refugees as well as those from population wars. According to the United Nations High Commissioner of Refugees, the world had 27.4 million refugees in 1995. This was 4.4 million higher than the year before and 17 million more than the preceding ten years. Another 20 million were refugees within their own countries.

Out of a global workforce of about two billion eight-hundred million people, at least 120 million are unemployed and another 700 million are under-employed or without enough income to meet basic human needs. A major reason for this is that in many countries there is not enough arable land or water to provide food for the people who live there. Nor is there enough available employment for landless people. This has been both a reason for economic migration and the tension leading to population wars.

An article by Hal Kane in a 1995 *World Watch* magazine said, "Apart from the long-established migratory pressures of war, persecution, and the pull of economic opportunity, migrants are now responding to scarcities of land, water, and food that are more widespread than ever before. They are leaving because of overcrowding in decrepit squatter settlements that now house huge numbers of people, because of post-Cold War changes in political climate, and because of widening disparities of income. This is why most of the world's migration has yet to happen."

An illustration of some of these problems appeared in the March 1, 1998, *Kansas City Star's* description of Burkino Faso, a "landlocked West African country slightly larger than Colorado, where women often walk miles every day to fetch water and firewood, and the average family earns less than $300 in a good year. . . . Last month Burkino Faso applied for emergency foreign aid to feed about 800,000 famished people left without food after a serious drought affected the main crops of sorghum, millet and corn."

Even in the Americas there are hundreds of thousands of economic refugees. More than one-and-a-half million refugees from Mexico, El

Salvador, Guatemala, and other countries below Mexico live within 25 miles of the United States, hoping to cross the border. Hundreds of thousands live in huts, makeshift tents, lean-tos, and caves without adequate sanitation, or health and law enforcement assistance. Estimates are that more than a million residents of Tijuana just south of San Diego live under these conditions. They and other millions are malnourished and many have communicable diseases, including AIDS. Their future seems dim.

Some of them are also refugees from earlier wars in Central America and Mexico, fought over control of land.

The most devastating population war in recent history was the war in Rwanda which began in 1994. It began in the most densely populated country in Africa, where virtually all arable land was in use by the mid-1980s.

Michael Renner of the World Watch Institute noted that in Rwanda "half of all farming took place on hillsides by the mid-80s, when overcultivation and soil erosion led to falling yields and a steep decline in total grain production."

In Rwanda there were 1,800,000 refugees living outside its borders in 1995, and close to one million Rwandans had been slaughtered.

The British medical journal, *The Lancet*, said Rwanda had the world's highest fertility rate and "the fact that any country could now be in intensely Catholic Rwanda's predicament is an indication of the world's and especially the Holy See's reluctance to face the issues of population control."

Renner noted that "The Hutu leaders that planned and carried out the genocide in 1994 relied strongly on heavily armed militias who were recruited primarily from the unemployed. "These were the people who had insufficient land to establish and support a family of their own and little prospect of finding jobs outside agriculture. Their lack of hope for the future and low self esteem were channeled by the extremists into an orgy of violence against those who supposedly were to blame for these misfortunes."

Population wars are caused not only by shortages of land but by scarcity of water. Sandia Postel in her 1992 book, *Last Oasis: Facing Water Scarcity*, indicates that early in the 90s, twenty-six countries with combined population of about 230 million people had water scarcity.

The shortage of water in the Mideast is illustrative. "No matter what progress irrigated agriculture makes, Jordan's natural water at this pace will be exhausted in 2010," predicted Elias Salameh, founder and former director of the University of Jordan's Water Research and Study Center, according to the May 14, 1992, *Washington Post*. "Jordan then will be totally dependent on rain water and will revert to desert. Its ruin will destabilize the entire region."

Salameh continued, "None of the regional countries -- Egypt, Israel, Jordan, Syria, Saudi Arabia or the Gulf Emirates -- can be self-sufficient in food in the foreseeable future, if ever. All Middle East economies must be restructured away from agriculture because of a lack of water."

The economic and military problems discussed all too briefly above require changes in our approach to social ethics and to our national politics. The facts of overpopulation and depletion of natural resources must be faced.

It is no secret that the Vatican has been one of the most adamant opponents of contraceptive birth control and worldwide family planning for decades. An article in the April 4, 1998, *Pittsburgh Tribune Review* said, "In the early 1980s, Pope John Paul II came to Nairobi and counseled Kenyans, whose population at that time was the fastest-growing in Africa, probably in the world, to 'be fruitful and multiply.'"

The *New York Times* reported on May 29, 1992, "In preparation for next month's Earth Summit in Rio de Janeiro, Vatican diplomats have begun a campaign to try to insure that the gathering's conclusions on the issue of runaway population growth are not in conflict with the Roman Catholic teaching on birth control."

Time magazine of February 24, 1992, in a story entitled, "The U.S. and the Vatican on Birth Control" began with this sentence: "In response to concerns of the Vatican, the Reagan Administration agreed to alter its foreign aid program to comply with the church's teaching on birth control." And in July 1992, the Sierra Club attacked President Bush for vetoing "two foreign aid budgets in order to block all U.S. funding for the United Nations Fund for Population program" and linked Bush's policy to "the urging of the Vatican." The 1998 Republican-controlled Congress followed the same position by linking payment of the U.S. debt to the United Nations with a provision against funding family planning overseas of any government or private agency that was involved in funding or lobbying for abortion.

By contrast, the British medical journal, *The Lancet*, has said, "No country has achieved smaller families or low maternal mortality without access to safe abortion -- and none will in the foreseeable future."

There are also additional remedies such as recognizing that women worldwide are not the property of their husbands or fathers, but moral decision-makers with respect to their health, their lives and their future. Neither are they public property for governmental decisions that require them to become pregnant or remain pregnant against their will. Unless we recognize women's rights the dire consequences for life on the planet are enormous.

Jennifer Mitchell in the January/February 1998 *World Watch* wrote:

In the developing world, at least 120 million married women and a large undefined number of unmarried women want more control over their pregnancies, but cannot get family planning services. This unmet demand will cause about one third of the projected population growth in developing countries over the next fifty years, or an increase of about 1.2 billion people.

The World Health Organization estimates that 585,000 women die each year during pregnancy and childbirth. "The death toll," according to the 1997 World Watch *Vital Signs*, "underestimates the magnitude of the problem. For every maternal death as many as thirty women sustain oftentimes crippling and lifelong health problems related to pregnancy." Moreover, many of these deaths and lifelong health problems could have been prevented by access to family planning services, and safe, legal abortion.

There is more to this culture of death evident in the fact that more than 4.7 million people, most of them in southeast Asia and sub-Saharan Africa, contracted HIV in 1995, and 1.7 million died from AIDS in 1995. By 1998, these figures are significantly higher. The Vatican has also strongly opposed any funding of condoms to prevent disease. What this means is that the "pro-life" movement primarily sponsored by the Vatican is really a pro-death movement, not only because of population wars but because of its denial of reproductive freedom to women worldwide and its denial of condoms to prevent the spread of contagious disease.

The other major key to the solution of overpopulation and disease lies with the United States and the American people. We put our resources into weapons and provide tax breaks for huge multinational corporations and arms industries, with very little regard for their degradations of the environment, at home or abroad.

The United States provides many of the weapons used in population wars. The U.S. annually spends more than $450 million, and the Pentagon employs an arms sales staff of 6,395, to promote and service foreign arms sales. Major weapons-exporting firms contributed $14.8 million to Congressional candidates from 1990 to 1994, and over $500,000 to the Republican and Democratic parties for the 1996 Presidential election.

In the words of Omar Khayam, they, and we, "want to take the cash and let the credit go, nor heed the rumble of the distant drum."

With respect to Christian leadership, the fundamentalist and evangelical churches accept the Vatican's position on family planning services, or, like the mainline churches, are not politically active either to support family planning or reduction of arms and of poverty worldwide.

What does this acquiescence or silence mean in the face of the great future planetary catastrophe we all face?

ANALYSIS OF THE ROMAN CATHOLIC BISHOPS' NOVEMBER 1998 POLITICAL PASTORAL STATEMENT

The Catholic bishops in November 1998 made a new appeal to Catholic legislators designed to persuade or coerce them to end a woman's right to a legal abortion. This follows their 1975 "Pastoral Plan for Pro-Life Activities," a detailed blueprint of their political program for achieving dominance of American politics at national, state and local levels.

The 1975 plan was a political strategy for controlling Congress, the judiciary, and the presidency on the issue of abortion. Catholic writer Timothy Byrnes called it the most "focused and aggressive political leadership" ever exerted by the American hierarchy. It mobilized twenty major Catholic organizations, such as the Knights of Columbus, the Catholic press, the Catholic Physicians Guild and the Catholic Lawyers Association, and organized in each diocese a Pro-Life Committee and similar groups in each state and congressional district.

Their strategy to influence presidential appointments to the judiciary was so successful during the Reagan and Bush years that not one pro-choice judge was appointed and, today, over 70 percent of federal judges are anti-choice. They persuaded Reagan and Bush to follow a foreign policy against family planning and sent laity to organize Protestant evangelists and churches as "front groups" so as to avoid anti-Catholic criticism or knowledge that the bishops were managing their campaign. With the assistance of Jerry Falwell, Pat Robertson, the Christian Coalition, the Mormons, the Southern Baptist Convention and others, they have effectively controlled the House of Representatives on this issue, functioning through such key laymen as Henry Hyde (R., IL) and Christopher Smith (R., NJ).

In spite of their massive campaign, they have not succeeded in getting a constitutional amendment to ban all abortions or even all late-term abortions, for which they invented the term "partial birth abortions."

Although they have gained political victories in many states, they have not established full theocratic control. In large part this was due to American Catholic voters who supported both a pro-choice president and many

Reprinted by permission from The Churchman/Human Quest, *March-April 1999.*

members of the House and Senate. Now, however, if the Catholic hierarchy is to succeed, it must convince Catholic politicians and voters to do what the Vatican wants, and what it failed to do in Europe, where predominantly Catholic Italy, France, Spain, Austria, and other countries have legalized abortion despite strong Vatican efforts to the contrary.

It is essential to know that the Vatican position against abortion also bans any contraception that functions after intercourse to prevent implantation. Moreover, if they can successfully control votes on abortion and contraception, the same political machine can end separation of church and state, use taxes to finance parochial schools, and prevent equal rights for women as well as others.

Analysis of the Bishops' 1998 Pastoral

The 27-page Catholic bishops' statement, "Living the Gospel of Life," begins with a statement of the pope and also the bishops as to why American political, economic and cultural power, which have "reshaped the world" should now accept Vatican morality and lead the world in that direction.

This document is factually incorrect at essential main points.

Distortion of History

The bishops try to appeal to American Catholics' pride in our country's history: "As Americans, as Catholics, and as pastors of our people, we . . . call our fellow citizens back to our country's founding principles, and most especially to renew our national respect for the rights of the unborn."

Fact: In colonial America and even after the Constitution was adopted, English Common Law was in effect. It permitted abortion before fetal movement or "quickening," which was generally detectable after about the 16th week of pregnancy. The Articles of Confederation, the Declaration of Independence and the Constitution have no mention of any rights for the unborn. There were no laws with respect to abortion in the U.S. prior to 1821 in Connecticut, 1827 in Illinois, and 1830 in New York.

A New Jersey case, *State vs. Murphy*, explained the purpose of the state statute of 1849. That decision said: "The design of the statute was not to prevent the procuring of abortions, so much as to guard the health and life of the mother against the consequences of such attempts . . . It is immaterial whether the fetus is destroyed or whether it has quickened or not. . ."[1]

America's founding principles made no reference to rights of the unborn, as the bishops assert. It is dishonest to attempt to make the phrase in the Declaration of Independence about the "laws of Nature and of Nature's God" mean what the pope means by natural law. It is also dishonest to assert that "all men are created equal" refers to male and female fetuses, when it didn't even refer to slaves and women as having equal rights.

When the bishops also quote the phrase, "certain inalienable rights . . . Among these are life, liberty and the pursuit of happiness," they emphasize life for a fetus instead of the life and liberty of a woman to choose whether or not to continue a problem pregnancy. The authors of the founding documents of the United States did not even consider these words as dealing with fetal life or abortion.

A Sectarian Statement

The bishops state: "The inherent value of human life is not a sectarian issue any more than the Declaration of Independence is a sectarian creed."

Fact: The word "sectarian" refers to issues or actions that are fostered by church dogma on which some or all other religious groups differ. The Declaration of Independence is not a creed, but a political manifesto which referred to men (not the unborn) as having "inalienable" rights. The bishops' statement is sectarian in its reference to embryonic and fetal life and is not concerned with the life or health of a woman but only with the contents of her womb.

The bishops' statement, which is intended to implement papal doctrine, is also sectarian precisely because it is a statement by the Catholic hierarchy, not accepted by many Catholics and most Jews, Protestants and Humanists. The bishops also, again and again, direct it to Catholic members, Catholic politicians and voters, and invoke quotations from the pope. The statement also ends with a prayer to Mary, mother of the church.

Biblical Distortion

The bishops' statement quotes Jeremiah 1:5 at the very beginning. Jeremiah says, "Now the word of the Lord came to me saying, 'Before I formed you in the womb I knew you; before you were born, I consecrated you; a prophet to the nations I appointed you."

Fact: Jeremiah is making a claim about his credentials and authority to preach. He did not make a comment about whether God creates every conceptus, or has known us before we were conceived and, therefore, wills that every conceptus come to term.

Until the present abortion controversy, this passage was identified as a vocational call, having nothing to do with abortion. Later, in Jeremiah 15:10

and 20:17, Jeremiah regrets that he was born and that he did not die in his mother's womb.

The bishops should know that an important principle in understanding Scripture is exegesis: what does the writer say in context? Exegesis does not permit us to take a passage that deals with a specific situation or issue and turn it into a partisan or modern abortion text.

Jesus and Sanctity of Life

The bishops say Catholics should "recover their identity as followers of Jesus Christ and be leaders in the renewal of America's respect for the sanctity of life."

Fact: Jesus never mentioned abortion or sanctity of life. Nowhere in the Scriptures is there any reference to sacredness or sanctity or respect for fetal life. The only reference that comes close to this is Luke 2:23: "Every male that opens the womb shall be called holy to the Lord."[2] It is characteristic of both Jewish and Christian Scripture that one must be born to be respected or to participate in the holy.

Just what does "sanctity of life" mean? Does it mean that all life must be treated with reverence and respect? Does it mean that embryonic life is more sacred than the life or health of the woman? The problem which cardinals and bishops do not face is that of conflict between existing persons and potential persons. They don't face the question of whether there should be a bias in favor of the woman. They promote a bias in favor of an embryo or fetus that may miscarry up to 50 percent of the time. What about a woman with diabetes, epilepsy or some other disease that would jeopardize her life if she continued a pregnancy to term? Is her life sacred?

Catholic ethicist Daniel Callahan refers to "the case of a mother with too many children and too few material, familial, social or psychological resources to care for them" and concludes that "the full human meaning of the act of abortion is preservation of the existing children."[3]

Apparently the bishops define "sanctity of life" as fetal life that is inviolable. This means that all other human rights are ignored by the need to preserve embryonic and fetal life. In other words, Vatican legalism does not permit an examination of the context in which pregnant women find themselves. For example, a mother with three or four children whose husband with a recent heart attack can no longer support the family and she has to do so. Or a woman with one disabled child who is told she is bearing another deformed fetus that will require full-time care. The bishops do not take responsibility for such problems. They won't even take such problem children into their parochial schools without complete government funding.

When the bishops launched the campaign against "partial birth abortions," they did not take into account that such late-term emergency abortions were performed on women who wanted a baby, many of them Catholics opposed to abortion. There are numerous case studies of such abortions, medically known as dilation and extraction (D & X), but one must suffice here:

Coreen Costello from Agoura, California, in April 1995 was pregnant with her third child. She and her husband found out that a lethal neuromuscular disease had left their much-wanted daughter unable to survive. Its body had stiffened and was frozen, wedged in a transverse position. In addition, amniotic fluid had puddled and built up to dangerous levels in Coreen's uterus. Devout Christians and opposed to abortion, the Costellos agonized for over two weeks about their decision and baptized the fetus in utero. Finally, Coreen's increasing health problems forced them to accept the advice of numerous medical experts that the intact dilation and extraction (D & X) was, indeed, the best option for Coreen's own health, and the abortion was performed. Later, in June 1996, Coreen gave birth to a healthy son.[4]

Again and again, the bishops try to associate their anti-abortion position with the Gospel. Although abortion was widely practiced in the ancient world, there is not one reference against abortion in the entire New Testament. Even in the Hebrew Scripture or Old Testament, the only reference to individual abortion is in Numbers 5, where God commanded an abortion with respect to an unfaithful wife. Elsewhere God is quoted as having ordered many hundreds of abortions. In Isaiah 13 and Hosea 13 there are references to "ripping up women with child" and destroying "the fruit of the womb."

When does human life begin?

The bishops state: "The point when human life begins is not a religious belief but a scientific fact."

Fact: Human life exists in the sperm and ovum. The real question is when does human life become a human being or person. It is misleading to speak of "a moment of conception" when sperm meets egg following sexual intercourse. Conception is not complete until the fertilized egg is implanted in the uterus, which generally occurs about 10 days to two weeks after ovulation. Up to 50 percent of fertilized eggs do not implant, and in those cases it is not possible to speak of conception. Except in cases of in vitro fertilization, it is impossible to know that fertilization has taken place until implantation occurs.

Charles Gardner, who did his doctoral research on the genetic control of brain development at the University of Michigan Medical School's Department of Anatomy and Cell Biology, says, "The 'biological' argument that a human being is created at fertilization . . . comes as a surprise to most embryologists . . . for it contradicts all that they have learned in the past few decades."

Gardner notes that "in humans when two sibling embryos combine into one, the resultant person may be completely normal. If the two original embryos were determined to become particular individuals, such a thing could not happen. The embryos would recognize themselves to be different . . . and would not unite. But here the cells seem unaware of any distinction between themselves . . . The only explanation is that the individual is not fixed or determined at this stage."

Gardner also notes, "The fertilized egg is clearly not a prepackaged human being . . . Our genes give us a propensity for certain characteristics. So how can an embryo be a human being? . . . The information to make an eye or a finger does not exist in the fertilized egg. It exists in the positions and interactions of cells and molecules that will be formed at a later date."

Such research and discoveries lead to the conclusion that it is a developmental process taking about nine months that produces a human being or person. Therefore, the Vatican idea that a human exists at conception is a theological statement rather than a medical or scientific fact.

Gardner concludes that "fertilization, the injection of sperm DNA into the egg, is just one of the many small steps toward full human potential. It seems arbitrary to invest this biological event with any special moral significance. . . . It would be a great tragedy if, in ignorance of the process that is the embryo, state legislators pass laws restricting the individual freedom of choice and press them upon the people. The embryo is not a child. It is not a baby. It is not yet a human being."[5]

The Human Person

The bishops attack abortion as a "violation of the human person's most fundamental right -- the right to life." In fact, the bishops use "human life" and "person's life" interchangeably, even though the Vatican has not proclaimed an embryo or conceptus as a person. When is there a person? The brain is the crucial element of personhood, and a statement by 167 scientists indicates that "at about 28 weeks of gestation, brain development is marked by the sudden emergence of dendritic spines in the neo-cortex. Dendritic spines are essential components in the brain's cellular circuitry."[6]

Michael V.L. Bennett, chair of the Department of Neuroscience, Albert Einstein College of Medicine, wrote that "personhood goes with the brain and does not reside within the recipient body . . . There is none, not heart, kidney, lung or spleen that we cannot transplant, do without, or replace artificially. The brain is the essence of our existence. It cannot be transplanted."[7]

The Right to Life

The bishops speak about the "most fundamental right -- the right to life." In discussing this claim we must distinguish between a virtue, that is, doing something that may be desirable, and a right. If I am walking along a river and someone who can't swim falls or jumps in, she/he cannot claim that I must jump in to rescue her because she has a right to life. The mere fact that I ought to rescue another does not give that person or society a right against me.

The common law rule is that we have no duty to save the life of another person unless we voluntarily undertake such an obligation, as a lifeguard does in contracting to save lives at a swimming pool. No woman should be required to give up her life or health or family security to save the life of a fetus that is threatening her well-being. At the very least she is entitled to self-defense. Moreover, the act of intercourse is not a contract for pregnancy. Even less should the act of rape be regarded as a guarantee, to a resulting fetus, of the right to life.

Thou Shalt Not Kill

The bishops also appeal to the Sixth [or Fifth, depending on which version one refers to] of the Ten Commandments: "Thou shalt not kill." This was and is not applicable to fetal life but refers to those who are human persons, as do all the other commandments. However, in the same Mosaic law there is a listing of those to be put to death, such as those who curse father or mother. In so doing the bishops show their lack of regard for biblical admonition and are special pleaders for a position not validated in the Bible.

Ideology

The bishops refer to "idolatry of the self" or the placing of "my needs, my appetites, my choices to the exclusion of moral restraints." Actually, the bishops are engaging in fetal idolatry in absolutizing the sacredness of the fetus. Like an Old Testament idol, the fetus is something for which a sacrifice must be offered. Fetal idolatry denies a woman's right to control her body, her life, her destiny, which must be sacrificed to an embryo or fetus once she is pregnant.

Fetal idolatry is bolstered by two other idolatries. One is patriarchy and the second in religious hierarchy. Both are evident in the subordination of women to men, who have historically made political, economic and religious decisions for women. In this "sanctity" of fetal life, a male hierarchy is attempting to make a virtue out of women's subordination. For years the Republican Party platform echoed Vatican doctrine with this statement: "The unborn child has a fundamental right to life that cannot be infringed." This means, as does the bishops' statement, that men and fetuses have a fundamental right to life, but pregnant women do not.

Endnotes

[1] 27 N.J.L. (3 Dutcher) 1858 at 114-115.
[2] *Revised Standard Version*, also *King James* and *Phillips*.
[3] *Abortion, Law, Choice and Morality*, p. 428.
[4] The author is indebted to Planned Parenthood of Kansas City for access to their files.
[5] "Is an embryo a Person?" *The Nation*, Nov. 13, 1989.
[6] Amicus Curiae Brief of 167 Distinguished Scientists and Physicians, including 11 Nobel Laureates, at 10-12 William Webster vs. Reproductive Health Services, 492 U.S. 490 (1989) No. 88-605).
[7] Michael V.L. Bennett, "Personhood from a Neuroscientific Perspective," in *Abortion Rights and Fetal Personhood*, 77, Edd Doerr and James W. Prescott, eds., 1990.

ABORTION: A NONVIOLENT CHOICE

Why have most major U.S. peace organizations committed to non-violence *not* joined the anti-abortion movement? Is it perhaps because women -- and some men -- in these movements realize that when women are not free to make choices with respect to pregnancy, they often experience violence?

In our society, there are at least two types of violence against women. The overt type includes such acts as rape, spouse abuse and sexual harassment. The covert type (frequently hidden behind the myth that motherhood and care of children define a woman's role) has been institutionalized in religious, economic and political systems, and enforced by legislation and by custom.

One illustration of this covert violence against women is inherent in what is, in fact, compulsory pregnancy. A woman made pregnant through rape or incest has no choice; others have controlled her body and well-being. Another no-choice situation involves women compelled to remain pregnant because of a failed contraceptive. (The failure rate of "natural family planning" runs as high as 35 percent.) Compulsory pregnancy, like compulsory labor (labeled by the Constitution as "involuntary servitude") is a denial of freedom and hence a form of violence.

There is violence also in the idea embodied in some legislation that a woman may have an abortion only if the pregnancy endangers her life. This means that any damage to a woman's health short of death is "acceptable" violence; suffering brought on by exacerbation of existing health problems such as diabetes or heart disease and the shortening of her life thereby are "acceptable" violence. The imperiling of a woman's mental health is also a type of violence.

What about fetal deformity? Legislators considering banning of abortions do not generally consider this an exception, however severe. Yet such a birth, besides being a serious psychological blow to a woman, might involve for her full-time child care for twenty or more years.

There is also covert violence in the idea that women should not have sexual intercourse if they don't want children. An act of sexual intercourse is not an implied contract to have children. While this may be the belief of those who accept the doctrine that every sexual act must be open to procreation, it would be violent for any government to decide that such a sectarian doctrine

---

Reprinted by permission from Courage, *the newsletter of the Loretto Women's Network, October 1990.*

should be enforced against any one, Catholic or non-Catholic, who does not accept that teaching.

When it is assumed that a woman, by the fact of intercourse, "asks for" pregnancy, there is an element of puritanical punishment or revenge in the idea that, once pregnant, she must be compelled to remain so. The man, who is equally responsible for the pregnancy is not similarly "punished."

Adoption is not a nonviolent answer. The argument of those who believe in compulsory pregnancy is that, if the fetus is unwanted or endangers the health of a woman, she must nevertheless give birth and then give up the child for adoption. In effect this would mean that a woman who does not want a child, but who becomes pregnant from rape, incest, failed contraception or ignorance about her reproductive processes must serve as a surrogate mother without pay for the benefit of another person or couple. Forcing women to bear children they do not want and cannot support or care for, and then to go through the trauma of giving them away is a form of violence. And what of the unwanted child given up for adoption who may not ever find a home because it is not white or healthy.

The abortion controversy itself also contributes to ineffective methods of birth control and hence to abortion. Organized boycotts by church and anti-abortion groups have been a contributing factor in reducing from nine to one the number of drug firms [in the U.S.] engaged in contraceptive research. Congress has also been lobbied to reduce or eliminate funding for research on any methods for preventing pregnancy except "natural family planning." The absence of effective and safe contraceptives from which men and women can choose does not contribute to nonviolent alternatives to abortion.

Violence occurs in the requirement of parental notification by teenagers before they can get an abortion. Most teenagers who seek an abortion do consult at least one parent, but some feel unable to do so for various reasons, such as fear of being beaten or killed, exiled from the family, or psychologically rejected. At least one teenager to my knowledge committed suicide in the mistaken notion that she could not face her parents.

Incest is one of the reasons for teenagers not consulting parents about pregnancy. The National Center for Child Abuse and Neglect states that there are at least 100,000 cases of incest-rape each year. Some estimates are as high as 250,000. Between 12 and 24 percent of incest victims become pregnant. Exposing abuse within one's family brings both trauma and reprisals. So the insistence on laws requiring parental consent is a form of violence against young women.

A proposal that has some influence with those who seek nonviolent solutions is the "consistent life ethic," linking opposition to abortion, the death penalty and war. At first glance, this seems a logical unity against violence. It is, however, not consistent in respecting the lives of women faced with a dangerous pregnancy. Like other absolute rules, there is no recognition of a conflict of life with life. Therefore, embryonic life is given priority over the life of the existing woman. Moreover, this idea, which originated with a member of the Catholic hierarchy, Cardinal Bernardin, treats women who have abortions differently from those who participate in war or in the death penalty. Women who have abortions are automatically excommunicated; judges, juries and executioners who inflict the death penalty, and CIA agents or military personnel who kill again and again are not excommunicated or held up to scorn. Thus, the "consistent life ethic" is chiefly directed against pregnant women, and is a form of covert violence.

The complexities of the abortion controversy have kept nonviolent groups from condemning what is clearly the termination of potential human beings through abortion. One peace-minded group, the General Committee of the Friends' Committee on National Legislation, as early as 1975 adopted the following statement that recognizes the dilemma in the abortion controversy:

Members of the Religious Society of Friends have an historic position and witness in opposition to killing of human beings, whether in war or capital punishment or personal violence. On the basis of this tradition, some Friends believe that abortion is always wrong.

Friends also have a tradition of respect for the individual and a belief that all persons should be free to follow their own consciences and the leading of the Spirit. On this basis, some Friends believe that the problem of whether or not to have an abortion, at least in the early months of pregnancy, is one primarily of the pregnant woman herself, and that it is an unwarranted denial of her moral freedom to forbid her to do so.

We do not advocate abortion. We recognize there are those who regard abortion as immoral while others do not. Since these disagreements exist in the country in general as well as within the Society of Friends, neither view should be imposed by law upon those who hold the other.

"Recognizing that differences among Friends exist, nevertheless we find general unity in opposing the effort . . . to say that abortion shall be illegal.

ABORTION: A CHRISTIAN ETHICAL PERSPECTIVE

The tragedy of an unwanted pregnancy that threatens a woman's life or health existed in the ancient world as it does today. At the time the Bible was written, abortion was widely practiced in spite of heavy penalties. The Assyrian code prohibited abortion with this statement: "Any woman who causes to fall what her womb holds . . . shall be tried, convicted and impaled upon a stake and shall not be buried." In Assyria the fetus was given more value than the woman.

The Bible on Abortion

Although the Hebrews were influenced by many of the laws of their Assyrian, Sumerian, and Babylonian neighbors, all of which forbade abortion, the Hebrew scriptures had no laws forbidding abortion. This was chiefly because the Hebrews placed a higher value on women than did their neighbors. There are, however, some references to the termination of pregnancy. Exod. 21:22-25 says that if a pregnant woman has a miscarriage as a result of injuries she receives during a fight between two men, the penalty for the loss of the fetus is a fine; if the woman is killed, the penalty is "life for life." It is obvious from this passage that men whose fighting had caused a woman to miscarry were not regarded as murderers because they had not killed the woman. The woman, undeniably, had greater moral and religious worth than did the fetus.

There is also reference in the Mosaic law to what is now called "abortion on request." Num. 5:11-31 indicates that if a husband suspects his wife is pregnant by another man, the "husband shall bring his wife to the priest," who shall mix a drink intended to make her confess or be threatened with termination of her pregnancy if she has been unfaithful to her husband.

Aside from these passages, the Bible does not deal with the subject of abortion. Although both Testaments generally criticize the practices of the Hebrews' neighbors, such as idol worship and prostitution, as well as various immoral acts committed in their own land, there is no condemnation or prohibition of abortion anywhere in the Bible in spite of the fact that techniques for inducing abortion had been developed and were widely used by

Published originally by the Religious Coalition for Reproductive Choice, © *1996. Reprinted by permission.*

the time of the New Testament.

When Does Life Begin?

A key question in the abortion controversy is, "When does human life begin?" The Bible's clear answer is that human life begins at birth, with the first breath. In Gen. 2:7, God "breathed into his nostrils the breath of life and man became a living being" (in some translations, "a living soul"). The Hebrew word for human being or living person is *nephesh*, which is also the word for "breath*ing*." *Nephesh* occurs hundreds of times in the Bible as the identifying factor in human life. This is consistent with the opinion of modern medical science. A group of 167 distinguished scientists and physicians told the Supreme Court in 1989 that "the most important determinant of viability is lung development," and that viability is not achieved significantly earlier than at twenty-four weeks of gestation because critical organs, "particularly the lungs and kidneys, do not mature before that time."[1]

In the Christian scriptures the Incarnation, or "the Word made flesh," was celebrated at the time of Jesus' birth, not at a speculative time of conception. We follow the biblical tradition today by counting age from the date of birth rather than from conception, a date people do not know or seek to estimate. The state issues birth certificates, not conception certificates.

The Vatican's assumption that human life begins at conception--which is derived from Greek philosophy, rather than the Bible--implies that a human being is created at a specific moment instead of by a process that takes about nine months. The Vatican also assumes that each person remains essentially what he or she was at conception, as if genes were omnipotent.

A person is more than a collection of cells created by 46 chromosomes. As the geneticist Charles Gardner observed, "Both the maternal environment outside the embryo and an unpredictable randomness inside the embryo have their effect" at every stage of development, as evidenced by the fact that genetically identical embryos will not make identical human beings."[2]

To focus on the biological realities of genes and chromosomes present at conception or to think of personhood solely in maternalistic or biological terms neglects the spiritual nature and characteristics of humans, whom the Bible describes as created "in the image of God" (Gen. 1:26-27). This description refers not to biological similarities but to the abilities to love and to reason; to the capacity for self-awareness and transcendence; and to the freedom to choose, rather than to live by instinct.

The brain is crucial to such human abilities. Michael V.L. Bennett, Chair of the Department of Neuroscience, Albert Einstein College of Medicine, said, "Personhood goes with the brain and does not reside within the recipient body," although the body "is necessary for brain function." He asserted, "There is nothing, not heart, kidney, lung, or spleen that we cannot transplant, do without, or replace artificially. The brain (which cannot be transplanted) is the essence of our existence."[3] The 167 scientists and physicians mentioned above said, "It is not until sometime after 28 weeks of gestation that the fetal brain has the capacity to carry on the same range of neurological activity as the brain in a full-term newborn."[4]

Fifty-one percent of all abortions in the United States occur before the 8th week of pregnancy; more than 91 percent occur before the 12th week (in the first trimester); and more than 99 percent occur before 20 weeks, which is about 4 weeks before the time of viability (when 10 to 15 percent of fetuses can be saved by intensive care). In such cases of early abortion there is no fetal neocortex, and hence no pain. However, every termination of potential human life presents a moral problem and can be justified only by the damage to living persons that may result from an unacceptable pregnancy.

Contraception (birth control), the practice of which can greatly reduce the number of abortions, involves the prevention of conception, ovulation, or implantation in the uterus. The Vatican's position that all sexual activity must allow the possibility of procreation has led the antiabortion movement to be silent about contraception as a way to prevent the need for abortion. Other groups, including the Roman Catholic bishops, have exerted pressure to minimize or prevent research on new methods of contraception. The Vatican's idea that a human being exists at a particular moment during or immediately following intercourse has led virtually all antiabortion groups to oppose the prevention of implantation. The official position of the Vatican is that of advocating "natural family planning," the least effective method of birth control with a failure rate of 20 to 35 percent. It requires up to 17 days of abstinence from sexual relations each month. (The period of abstinence must include not only the days of a woman's fertile period, but extra days to allow for the durability of sperm within the female body.) The argument that conception is a more crucial step in the birth process than implantation is irrelevant. Conception is not complete until the fertilized egg is implanted in the uterus, which generally occurs about ten days to two weeks after ovulation. Up to 50 percent of fertilized eggs do not implant, and in those cases it is impossible to speak of conception. Except in cases of *in vitro* fertilization, it is impossible to know that fertilization has taken place until implantation occurs.

Of the fertilized eggs that are implanted, between 20 percent and 50 percent are miscarried. If objections to the prevention of implantation are based on the assumption that this is taking life, then nature or God is the greatest killer, because there are more spontaneous preventions of implantation than there are medical preventions. In other words, it is not God's will that every conception should eventuate either in implantation or in birth. This argument is consistent with our assertion that a fetus, as well as a fertilized egg, is a potential rather than an actual human being.

Actually, those who claim that a human being exists at conception are guilty of *prolepsis*, a term defined in *Webster's Dictionary* as "an anticipating, especially the describing of an event as if it had already happened."[5] This type of anticipation is being practiced by those who speak of the few cells that after conception or a fetus in the early trimesters as "a baby" or "an unborn child."

Do the Born and the Unborn Have Equal Value?

Some years ago at a meeting of the American Society of Christian Ethics, a workshop was confronted with the case of a 3-year-old child and an 18-week fetus, both with a dread disease for which there was only one injection of medicine in Chicago. The Chicago airports had been shut down by a blizzard, preventing the doctors from obtaining more of the medicine. We unanimously concluded that the child should get the injection. The moral difference is that the child is among us in a way that the fetus is not. The child's claim is based on relationship, rather than on a legal point of birth.

Although the Roman Catholic hierarchy strongly opposes intentional abortion, in practice it sometimes recognizes the priority of the woman over the fetus, as is evident in the following excerpt from a U.S. Catholic Conference publication:

> Operations, treatments and medications, which do not directly intend termination of pregnancy but which have as their purpose the cure of a proportionately serious pathological condition of the mother, are permitted when they cannot be safely postponed until the fetus is viable, even though they may or will result in the death of the fetus.[6]

The Roman Catholic Church argues that in this situation, although the death of the fetus is foreseen, it is not intended, because the intention is to preserve the health and the life of the woman. Is it not reasonable to assert that the intention of most women who choose abortion is to preserve their health and well-being, not to "kill" the fetus, although its death may be foreseen? In such situations, the fetus does not have equal value with the mother, and allowing the fetus to be lost is not the same as permitting the woman carrying the fetus to die or otherwise suffer.

Judaism generally views the fetus as a part of its mother. Just as a person may choose to sacrifice a limb or organ to be cured of a malady, so may the fetus be removed for the sake of the pregnant woman.

Isaac Klein, a 20th-century Conservative rabbi, elaborated on a ruling of Maimonides against a "pursuer" that is comparable to the law of self-defense: "Since the child causing a difficult birth and threatening the woman's life is regarding as one pursuing her and trying to kill her it may rightly be aborted."

Neither Anglo-Saxon law nor the U.S. Constitution has ever given a fetus the same legal status as a woman. Until a baby is born there is only a potential person. When abortion was illegal, it was viewed as a felony rather than a homicide. The fetus has always been a potential rather than an actual person.[7]

What right does a woman have to an abortion? One answer is that the rights of living persons takes precedence over any rights of potential persons, just as immediate or present needs take precedence over future or potential needs. This question can also be restated: What right does anyone have to impose mandatory pregnancy on a woman? The ethical question is not whether abortion can be justified, but whether we focus on an embryo or fetus as the object of value or whether we focus on the woman as a moral agent who must have freedom of choice.

The Freedom to Choose

When Moses asked God his name, God said, "I am who I am," or, in the future tense, "I will be who I will be." God is a free moral being whose actions are not determined by cause and effect. Humans made in the image of God are likewise moral beings precisely because they engage in free choice in all of their decisions.

A passage in Genesis describes humans as moral decision makers who, like God, know the difference between good and evil. Of all the animals in the Garden of Eden only one, the human being, was free to make choices. Humans were given the ability to choose between good and evil and, of course, the responsibility to face the consequences of their choices.

In the New Testament, there is an emphasis on the priesthood of all believers: "You are a chosen race, a royal priesthood, a holy nation, God's own people" (1 Pet 2:9). Each believer has direct access to God and has the ability to know and do God's revealed will. We are not bound by any natural law derived from Greek philosophy; neither are we bound by the ancient Jewish law or by any other legalism handed down by any religious or spiritual leader.

When Jesus said, "Man was not made for the Sabbath, the Sabbath was made for man" (Mark 2:27), he struck at the heart of legalism, or the imposition of rules for their own sake. The Bible tells us that we live by grace. This means that God acts within human beings to set us free and to enable us to assume responsibility for ourselves, our environment, and our future. If we make wrong choices, God's grace is available as judgment and forgiveness.

Humans, by the grace of God, have developed medicine, surgery, and psychiatry to prolong and enhance life. These same medical approaches can be chosen to prolong or enhance the life of a woman for whom a specific birth would be dangerous.

An area that has recently been emphasized in theological ethics is the integrity and welfare of women. Women, whose lives and freedom have been largely controlled by men for centuries, must make or be involved in decisions that affect their lives, their futures, their families. To refuse on principle to permit a woman to consider her life or welfare when it seems threatened by pregnancy is to say that only men are the recipients of God's grace in terms of freedom and responsibility. It is also to say that the primacy of the fetus's right to bodily life places all other considerations, including the health, worth, and dignity of women, on a lower level.

Doctrinal Issues

Catholic and Protestant doctrines differ in, among other things, the degree to which they are legalistic. The Catholic Church would have all obey the rules formulated by the Vatican, but Protestants believe that we are free by grace and justified by faith. The phrase "the sacredness of life" means one thing to Catholic bishops--that the life of the fetus is all-important--but to most Protestants and many others it means that there is a presumptive right to life that is not absolute but is conditioned by the claims of others. For us the right to life and the sacredness of life mean that there should be no absolute or unbreakable rules that take precedence over the lives of existing human persons.

The pro-life position is really a pro-fetus position, and the pro-choice position is really pro-woman. Those who take the pro-fetus position define the woman in relation to the fetus. They assert the rights of the fetus over the right of the woman to be a moral agent or decision maker with respect to her life, health, and family security.

The second doctrinal issue in both the abortion and birth-control controversies is who is to have the power to control procreation--women, in consultation with their partners and their physicians, or the church. The historic natural-law position of the Catholic Church was concerned not about feticide, but about the sin of sexuality if it interfered with procreation, as contraception and abortion do. The Pope and the bishops have been unable to persuade women to accept control by the church over their sexuality; their only hope for asserting that control is to persuade the state through political power to make a church sin into a secular crime. The low view of women that keeps them from being ordained and insists that their proper role is that of mother is not simply Catholic theology but fundamentalist political ideology, which is also anti-woman. The key term in the controversy is not simply "pro-life," but "pro-family," in which "family" is always defined as a patriarchal family.

As theologian Rosemary Reuther has pointed out:

It is not accidental that Catholic countries where both contraception and abortion are discouraged have higher abortion rates than countries where both are legal but where contraception is encouraged. It is also well known that Catholics in the United States have a higher proportion of abortions than Protestants and Jews. Why? Quite simply the combination of an anti-contraception culture, combined with hostility toward female sexuality and self-determination promotes the conditions of unchosen pregnancy and hence recourse to abortion as the unchosen but forced solution.

The Right of Privacy

The Supreme Court in its *Roe v. Wade* decision did not hold that women have a constitutional right to an abortion; it held that they have a constitutional right of privacy that permits them and their physicians to make decisions "including a woman's qualified right to terminate her pregnancy." The Court also held that during the last three months of pregnancy, the state, "in promoting its interest in the potentiality of human life, may, if it chooses, regulate, and even proscribe, abortion, except where necessary, in appropriate medical judgment, for the preservation of the life or health of the mother."

The right of privacy is the right to make personal choices without governmental supervision or dictation. The government exists to serve the people, not to dominate them. The government should not force women to bear children, to remain at home, to relinquish their careers, to accept welfare as the price of not working, or to be subjected to a higher mortality rate from coerced childbirth. Both the woman and her physician have the right to choose appropriate medical procedures for the health of the patient without government's dictating that one medical procedure is forbidden regardless of the consequences to the woman.

Rights, Obligations, and Laws

In answering the question, Is there a right to life in law or in biblical faith? we must distinguish between a virtue and a right. If I am walking along the bank of a river and someone who cannot swim falls or jumps in, it could be argued that I ought also to jump in to rescue the drowning person, even if my own life is thereby endangered. But the person who jumps or falls in cannot claim that I must jump in because that person has a right to life. The mere fact that rescuing another would be a virtuous choice does not give that other person a right to decide my actions.

The common-law rule is that we have no duty to save the life of another person unless we voluntarily undertake such an obligation, as a lifeguard does in contracting to save lives at a beach or swimming pool. Neither is there a biblical mandate that each of us is morally required to risk our lives to save the life of another. Jesus considered it highly exceptional and evidence of great love if "a man lay down his life for his friends" (John 15:13).

No one who has not willingly contracted to do so is legally or morally required to give his or her life, or to make large sacrifices of health or money, to save the life of another person. Even an identical twin is not legally required to donate a kidney or blood to save a sibling's life. The *virtue* of the Good Samaritan lay precisely in his doing something he was not *obligated* to do.

No woman should be required to give up her life, her health, or her family's security to save the life of a fetus that is threatening her well-being. At the very least she is entitled to self-defense. On the other hand, many women are willing to sacrifice their health and their future in order to have one or more children. The religious community that respects the freedom of women to make such a choice must respect equally their freedom to choose not to bear a child.

Laws cannot eliminate abortions. In Romania under Ceausescu, the Communist secret police checked monthly on all female workers under the age of 45 and monitored pregnant women; yet Romania outranked virtually all European nations in rates of abortion and abortion-related female deaths.[8] In Brazil, where abortion is illegal, there are twice as many abortions as in the United States, although Brazil's population is only half that of the United States. In Latin America, illegal abortion is the number-one killer of women between the ages of 15 and 39.[9] By contrast, in countries where abortion is legal, it is a medically safe procedure--11 times safer than childbirth.

The Cook County Hospital in Chicago, prior to the Supreme Court's decision legalizing abortion, admitted about 4,000 women each year for medical care following illegal abortions. After the decision, the hospital admitted fewer than five such cases a month.[10]

Reducing the Need for Abortion

Rather than pursuing laws banning abortion, which I believe would be as effective as passing laws against earthquakes, we should direct our energies toward reducing the need for the procedure. Supporters and opponents of legal abortion alike would agree that reducing the need for abortion, and thus the number of abortions performed, is a worthy goal.

Women do not engage in sexual intercourse or become pregnant in order to have abortions. Some women become pregnant unintentionally because of a lack of sex education. Increasing the availability of birth control information and contraceptives is a possible response to this problem.

Then there is the problem of contraceptive failure. The failure rate of barrier methods is in the 10 to 15 percent range, and of birth control pills 1 to 4 percent. Until a contraceptive that is 100 percent effective is developed and made widely available, we must provide support for victims of contraceptive failure. For some women, particularly those close to the poverty line who would be financially unable to care for an additional child without jeopardizing the very existence of their families, an unexpected pregnancy can be devastating. Free day care centers for children of working mothers, or a guaranteed annual income such as Milton Friedman and former senator Barry Goldwater once proposed, would remove some of the economic reasons for seeking abortions.

Another way the number of abortions could be reduced would be for society to provide ample facilities for the care of children with severe birth defects at no cost to the parents. For families unprepared or unable to devote the vast emotional and financial resources necessary to care for a severely handicapped child, such a program would present a compassionate and realistic alternative to abortion.

Finally, we must face the horrendous problems presented by rape and incest, both of which induce great suffering among their victims. The responsibility of men in sexual relationships must be stressed in the home, in schools, in our churches, and in our legal system. Our society must undertake strong educational and enforcement measures to reduce the tragedies of rape and incest and ensure the safety and dignity of American women.

The Need for Compassion

Many Christians are quick to condemn what they believe is immorality in others. Such people should be reminded that men and women sometimes find themselves caught in situations that they feel leave them no choice, and that we all need understanding, forgiveness, and compassion. All too often a young, physically and psychologically vulnerable woman must bear the entire physical, social, emotional, and financial cost of birth while the father of the child assumes no responsibility. A young woman in those circumstances needs the acceptance, love, and compassion of her parents, her pastor, and her community.

In the story of the woman who was about to be stoned because she had been caught in the act of adultery, Jesus expressed compassion and understanding when he said to the men, "Let him who is without sin cast the first stone," and to the woman, "Neither do I condemn you." Jesus was always more critical of sins of the spirit than sins of the flesh. That is why he spoke so compassionately to this woman, but so strongly to the self-righteous, legalistic men.

All of us who discuss ethics must learn from Jesus that it is not laws that make people good, but love, education, active concern for others, and forgiveness when others are found wanting.

Endnotes

[1.] Amicus Curiae Brief of 167 Distinguished Scientists and Physicians, Supreme Court of the U.S., October Term 1988, *William L. Webster v. Reproductive Health Ser*vices No. 88-605, p. 10.

[2.] Charles A. Gardner, *In These Times*, May 23-June 5, 1990.

[3.] *Abortion Rights and Fetal Personhood*, ed. by Edd Doerr and James W. Prescott (Long Beach, CA-Centerline Press, 1990), p. 77.

[4.] Amicus Curiae Brief, p. 14.

[5.] Webster's *New Universal Unabridged Dictionary* (New York: Simon and Schuster, 1979), p. 1439.

[6.] *Ethical and Religious Directives for Catholic Health Facilities*, Publications Office, United States Catholic Conference.

[7.] New York in its homicide statute defines a "person when referring to the victim of a homicide (as) a human being who has been born and is alive." (N.Y. Rev. Penal Law 125.05) The U.S. Constitution in the 14th Amendment also makes birth a prerequisite to citizenship.

[8.] Charlotte Hord et al., "Reproductive Health in Romania: Revising the Ceausescu Legacy," *Studies in Family Planning*, 22 (4) (July/August 1991): 231-239.

[9.] Toni Carabillo, *Abortion: For Survival, A Guide to the Videotape* (The Fund for the Feminist Majority, 1989), pp. 8-10.

[10.] Senator Charles Percy, *Congressional Record*, April 19, 1974.

CONSISTENT LIFE ETHIC:
VIOLENCE VS. WOMEN

A relatively new argument against abortion is now being advanced, known as the "consistent life ethic" or the "seamless garment." It is a two-edged sword used by Catholic pacifists who would like the "pro-life" Catholics also to oppose the death penalty, and at the same time would convince anti-war non-Catholics to oppose abortion.

This argument is based on certain long-held assumptions that everything from a fertilized egg to a 34-week fetus is an unborn child; that a human being exists immediately following the fertilization of the egg during intercourse, even though conception is actually not complete until the fertilized egg is implanted in the uterus, which may take as long as two weeks.

The idea that a baby exists in an embryo or an oak tree in an acorn is known as prolepsis, a propaganda term which Webster's dictionary defines as "an anticipating, especially the describing, an event as if it had already happened" when in fact it may be months away or may never happen. Even after conception, up to 50 percent are aborted by God or Nature as miscarriages.

There is a further assumption that every act of sexual intercourse is a contract for pregnancy, or, as popes have indicated, must be open to procreation. They ignore the fact that most people who engage in intercourse do not do so only when they plan a pregnancy. Pregnancy occurs from contraceptive failure as well as from wrong estimates of the fertility period and from unintended intercourse such as seduction or rape.

One major implication of this is a requirement of compulsory pregnancy for women. Unlike men, who are able to walk away from a pregnancy, women, under this belief, should not be allowed to do so, no matter what this does to their health, their vocation, the support of a parent or an invalid husband or dependent children.

Compulsory pregnancy is not just for nine months, but may involve years of care for a child, and even more years in the case of a deformed child or child with Downs Syndrome. Compulsory pregnancy is a form of slavery which those who claim the consistent life ethic are prepared to inflict on women for the sake of seeming to treat all life evenly, or for the sake of papal

Reprinted by permission from The Churchman/Human Quest, *March-April, 1998.*

law. There are even some women who call themselves "feminists for life" who justify compulsory pregnancy.

A second major part of the "consistent life ethic" is that its proponents do not advocate the prevention of pregnancy by contraceptive birth control, and hence do not deal in what is truly nonviolent prevention. The boycotting of any companies that do research on such prevention and legislation that prohibits funding for family planning and contraception makes abortion more likely.

There is no consistent life ethic that can honestly be claimed by the anti-abortionists. This is evident in the following question-answer statement in Father Patrick A. Finney's book, *Moral Problems in Hospital Practice*, published under the imprimatur of the Archbishop of St. Louis:

Q. If it is morally certain that a pregnant mother and her unborn child will both die if the pregnancy is allowed to take its course, but at the same time the attending physician is morally certain that he can save the mother's life by removing the inviable fetus, is it lawful for him to do so?

A. No, it is not. Such a removal of the fetus would be a direct abortion.

This is the serious fallacy not only in the so-called pro-life position but in the consistent life ethic. In other words, the pro-life position is really a pro-death sentence for women whose lives are at stake in a pregnancy, or whose health is such that compulsory pregnancy will lead to an early termination of lives.

Actually, the pro-life and consistent life ethic advocates are rationalizing violence by focusing only on the fetus as one that should be protected by some "sacredness of life" slogan. They ignore the covert violence against women by assuming that compulsory pregnancy is a virtue and that all pregnant women who do not want a child should be willing to accept violence to themselves in the interest of a sectarian ethic to which they may not subscribe. Whenever any group, however much it claims an interest in fetal life, is prepared to restrict the freedom of others for the sake of a sectarian dogma or "consistency," that is violence.

For example, to most anti-abortionists, any damage to a woman's health is "acceptable violence," suffering brought on by exacerbation of existing health problems such as diabetes or heart disease and the shortening of her life thereby are "acceptable violence." The imperiling of a woman's mental health is also a type of violence.

If violence is equated with the use of power to inflict pain, abortion (as practiced in the United States under the legal protection of present society as provided in *Roe v. Wade*) does not qualify as violence. The fetus does not feel pain before the development of the cerebrum, which does not exist until about the thirty-third week of gestation.

The Supreme Court has held that a woman is constitutionally entitled to have an abortion of a nonviable fetus. Therefore the physician performing second trimester abortions must first determine that the fetus is too underdeveloped to survive outside the womb.

After 24 weeks of pregnancy (the approximate date of viability and the beginning of the third trimester), the abortion procedure is not elective, but emergency, in that the fetus is gravely or fatally impaired or the woman's life or health is at risk. Ninety percent of all abortions are performed in the first trimester, and 99 percent within 20 weeks. No national data are available past 20 weeks, but the Alan Guttmacher Institute estimated, based on limited data collected by the U.S. Center for Disease Control, that approximately 320-600 abortions annually are performed after the 26th week of pregnancy.

There are certain conclusions to be drawn from this analysis. No legalistic formula such as a "consistent life ethic" is possible. Women as a group cannot be told that they have no freedom to decide their destiny. Many if not most women find abortion a positive or non-violent decision in the very early weeks of pregnancy and certainly in the prevention of implantation of a fertilized egg in the uterus by the "morning after" pill which pro-lifers generally oppose as abortion. Almost all emergency abortions are performed for women who wanted that child but faced a terrible crisis, like a fetus with no brain or other organs.

Certainly the emergency decisions made medically are as nonviolent as those made by persons who must lose a part of their body by amputation to survive. The following actual cases reveal both the regret and yet the positive acceptance of abortion as a solution to an emergency:

Tammy Watts, from Scottsdale, Arizona. In March, 1995, Tammy and her husband Mitch made the agonizing decision to end a wanted pregnancy at 28 weeks gestation. It would have been the first child. Her brain was severely damaged, and her skull had not formed in the back. Her liver and kidneys were oversized and already failing irreparably. Her bowel, bladder and intestines were formed on the outside of her body and had grown into a non-functioning mass of tissue. Doctors also told the couple that Tammy's health was at risk from a continued pregnancy, especially if the fetus died in utero.

Sophie Horak, from Batavia, Illinois. Sophie, the manager of a medical office, and her husband Bob, a firefighter, wanted a large family. In October of 1992 they were thrilled to learn that she was expecting their second child. In her fifth month of pregnancy, however, a routine ultrasound revealed an advanced and comprehensive case of diaphragmatic hernia. The surgery would not be possible, and Joey could not survive. Sophie and Bob wanted to spare their son any suffering, and agreed with their doctors' advice that terminating the pregnancy through intact D & E was the most appropriate medical option. After ending the pregnancy, the Horaks took their son home to Illinois for a Catholic funeral.

Eileen Sullivan, from Los Angeles, California. A Catholic with ten brothers and sisters, Eileen had long awaited her first child. She and her husband were devastated to discover, at 26 weeks of pregnancy, that testing revealed overwhelming and fatal abnormalities in their son, including an improperly formed brain, a malformed heart, no lungs, and a non-functioning liver. The severe anomalies were incompatible with life. Eileen had an intact D & E abortion.

Most people who read statistics about abortion or pro-life arguments are unaware of the personal and often tragic nature of the decisions actually made about abortion.

IDOLIZING THE FETUS

Opponents of abortion in America have attributed to fetal life a sacredness that is actually idolatry. The idol in Old Testament terms was inanimate, made of metal or stone. As such it was possible to attribute to it a tribe's cultural or group interests and to worship it instead of God. Idolatry is therefore the absolutizing of a cultural or belief system as if it is sacred or of divine origin and therefore more important than human personality; it is something to which sacrifice must be offered.

Fetal idolatry denies a woman's right to control her body, her life, her destiny, all of which must be sacrificed to an embryo or fetus once she is pregnant. The "right to life" movement succeeded in persuading or pressuring the Republican Party's platform committee to adopt this statement: "The unborn child has a fundamental right to life that cannot be infringed." This means that men and fetuses have a fundamental right to life but pregnant women do not.

In other words, a woman's life, health, or a family dependent upon her income are supposed to be beyond her control.

Fetal idolatry is bolstered by two other idolatries. One is patriarchy and the second, akin to it, is religious hierarchy. Both are evident in the subordination of women to men, who have historically made political, economic and religious decisions for women. Patriarchy is not just domination by men; it is clearly evident in clericalism, a religious system of domination which, in this context, is based on the attempt to make a virtue out of women's subordination.

The Roman Catholic Church and some Protestant churches, notably the Southern Baptist Convention, have elements of fetal, patriarchal and clerical idolatry, evident in their control by men, who refuse to ordain women or use gender-neutral language, and who oppose reproductive freedom for women.

Pope John Paul II, for example, in his encyclical *Laborem exercens*, has written that society's role is "to make it possible for a mother to devote herself to taking care of children and educating them in accordance with their needs . . . Having to abandon these tasks in order to take up paid work outside the home is wrong from the point of view of the good of society and of the family when it contradicts or hinders these primary goals of the mission of a mother."

This patriarchal approach is increasingly out of date as millions of married women have to work to help support a family; and fathers as well as

---

Reprinted by permission from The Churchman/Human Quest, *May-June 1998.*

mothers share in child care, household work and the education of children. Nevertheless patriarchy still exists.

Fetal idolatry or the denial of reproductive freedom to women is the major battleground issue for both patriarchal and clerical control of women. Unfortunately, unquestioning acceptance of an idolatry often leads to intimidation and even murder of those who take a different position. The idolatry of white superiority led to the violence and intimidation of blacks by the Ku Klux Klan and other groups when racial equality became an issue in our society. That violence, including lynching, burning of black churches, and separate accommodations on trains and in restaurants was, in fact, tolerated by others who did not personally engage in it.

Similar violence is being used today to bolster fetal idolatry. An editorial in the January 31, 1998, *Kansas City Star*, referring to the lethal bombing of an abortion clinic in Birmingham, Alabama, said:

> Acts of violence by persons opposed to abortion go back many years and have taken many forms, including shootings, bombings and fires at clinics. Before the latest bombings, five adults had lost their lives and others were injured. Last year alone 13 clinics were the targets of bombs and arson.

The editorial also said, "Others in the anti-abortion movement acted as if this murder and maiming were acceptable ways to protest against laws that protect women's access to abortion clinics."

There is much more evidence of violence. During the past 20 years there have been over 1,700 attacks against reproductive health clinics and there is no evidence that major religious leaders of the "pro life" movement have engaged in any effort to stop the violence. Women have also been imprisoned on buses and cars and harassed by "Operation Rescue" groups as they enter clinics.

Susie Blackmun, the daughter of Supreme Court Justice Harry Blackmun who wrote the Court's opinion in the *Roe v. Wade* decision, described tens of thousands of hate-filled letters sent to her father. "The death threats cost Dad his freedom to drive; he had to be chauffeured to and from work by Court police. When he traveled, U.S. marshals accompanied him. . . . they sometimes camped out in the driveway when he stayed with us. If we ate at a restaurant they sat at the next table."

A Boulder, Colorado, physician, Dr. Warren M. Hern, has to work behind layers of bullet proof windows after five shots were fired through the front windows of his office. In 1989 "Operation Rescue" leader Randall Terry with his followers gathered in front of his office while Terry publicly prayed for the doctor's execution. In 1993, following the assassination of Dr. Gunn, Terry in his broadcast publicly called for Hern's assassination. Dr. George Tiller was shot the next week in Wichita, and on January 22, 1995, the American Coalition of Life Activists announced a hit-list of the first thirteen doctors they wanted eliminated.

Dr. Malcolm Potts, Professor of Population and Family Planning at the School of Public Health at the University of California at Berkeley wrote:

> The right to life warriors who have slain health professionals working in abortion clinics are behaving exactly like those who fought in religious wars four hundred years ago. The idea of respecting those whose beliefs are different and even (most difficult of all) fighting to preserve the rights of others to practice a set of beliefs you yourself reject, is a noble idea. But this noble idea is forever threatened by the brute temptation to coerce others to your beliefs by the sword, the noose or the prison cell.

No pro-choice organization or individual, by contrast, has called for or practiced violence. It is the toleration and even practice of violence by Right-to-Lifers that is one aspect of idolatry. Fetal life is such a "sacred" value that existing persons who differ are threatened and killed.

Further evidence of fetal idolatry is the priority given to fetal life over the very life of the woman. This is evident in Father Patrick Finney's book, *Moral Problems in Hospital Practice*, published under the imprimatur of the Archbishop of St. Louis, using a question-answer form:

Q. If it is morally certain that a pregnant mother and her unborn child will both die, if the pregnancy is allowed to take its course, but at the same time the attending physician is morally certain that he can save the mother's life by removing the inviable fetus, is it lawful for him to do so?

A. No, it is not. Such a removal of the fetus would be a direct abortion.

In other words, when this religious law is carried over into politics, the deprivation of liberty for women is a political statement that their lives are less important than religious legalism.

Fetal idolatry is also evident in the idea of compulsory pregnancy. The right to life movement assumes that women's bodies are in effect public property. Once they are pregnant they must remain so, no matter what happens to a woman's life, health, family, other children, or her vocation. In other words, the "pro-lifers" insist that women whose rights are legally recognized in other contexts must be subordinated to a fetus whose rights are not recognized legally. If the right to life movement should win, women who have abortions and medical personnel who provide them would become criminals. Fetal idolatry shows no mercy. It assumes that sexual intercourse is a contract for pregnancy, although there are ample studies that reveal that women do not always choose intercourse, but are forced into it, in or out of marriage. One of these appears in Diane Russell's *Rape in Marriage*.

Those who insist that women who marry surrender their right to control when, where and whether to have intercourse, with or without contraception, are simply insisting that marriage is a patriarchal institution and not a relationship of equality.

Fetal idolatry, when contrasted with attitudes toward war, is wanting in consistency. The "pro-life" advocates do not publicly seek disarmament or even the abandonment of nuclear weapons or land mines, which kill children and women, many of them no doubt pregnant. They do not concern themselves with persuading the United States to ratify the Convention on the Rights of the Child, or with the fact that as many as 250,000 children, some as young as eight years old, are serving in government armies or armed rebel groups around the world.

Those involved in fetal idolatry generally do not even try to prevent unwanted pregnancies either by promoting the use of contraceptives during sexual intercourse or afterward to prevent implantation of the fertilized egg in the uterus. In fact, the Vatican's opposition to abortion also bans the use of contraceptives.

One of the major critiques of idolatry about unborn life is its lack of concern for the abundant or purposeful life to which all of us should be called. No one of us should be an unwanted child or have to experience emotional abandonment or lack of compassion and love in childhood. Yet unwanted pregnancies, especially involving school-age children unprepared for family responsibility are occurring by the thousands each year. Some are produced as the result of consensual sex, but many are the result of rape and incest.

The Alan Guttmacher Institute reported in 1996 that 7 in 10 women who had sex before age 14, and 6 in 10 of those who had sex before age 15 report having had sex involuntarily.

A federally funded 1992 study of 4,000 women projected that some one million children are raped every year. The study was done by the National Victims Center, a private advocacy organization.

An article in the August 9, 1993, *In These Times* states that "of some 5,000 births among California junior high school girls ages 11-15, only 7 percent were fathered by junior high boys. Four in ten were fathered by high school age boys 16-18, and more than half by post-high school age adult men ages 19 and older. Male partners of mothers age 12 and younger averaged 22 years of age. The author, Mike Males, also asserts that there is clear correlation between poverty and teen pregnancy. Mississippi, with "a 1990 per capita income of $12,735, has a youth childbearing rate three times higher than Connecticut" where per capita income is $25,358, and Los Angeles' poorest neighborhoods have teen pregnancy rates 20 times higher than its richest neighborhood."

He concludes that "teen pregnancy is not simply the result of dumb, immoral, ignorant or careless kids. Rather, early parenthood is an index of the levels of poverty, abuse and bleak opportunities afforded young women and their efforts to escape their harsh conditions by alliances with older partners -- a survival strategy."

We do not know how many of these teen-age women sought abortions or how many gave birth to children who also face poverty, abuse, or other harsh conditions. We should know that the idolatry that tries to prevent contraception in circumstances such as these condemns babies to the same circumstances their parents had to face. Fetal idolatry that in itself is immoral, also has tragic implications for society as a whole.

ABORTION AS A POSITIVE MORAL CHOICE

The violent arm of the right-wing anti-abortion movement is having a field day in the United States, not only with violence against doctors and clinic workers, but now with anthrax threats and hoaxes. At least twenty abortion clinics and other buildings nationwide received anthrax threats in February [of 1999].

The following description in the February 23 [1999] *Kansas City Star* indicates what happens when such a threat is received: "Emergency workers, more than 100 strong, swarmed over the Planned Parenthood clinic in midtown on Monday; hazardous material technicians laboring in white safety suits, police diverting traffic for blocks around the clinic, firefighters and rescue workers pouring in from four cities.

"Inside the clinic 27 persons were stripped and scrubbed with a mixture of bleach and soap, all the result of an anonymous letter" which "contained a note . . . stating that the person reading it had just been exposed to anthrax."

In 1997 "Kansas City was part of the first group of cities to receive new training against terrorism, including anthrax threats. The city has gathered millions in federal grants to train emergency workers and buy special equipment." So when there is a threat, even a hoax, the people who make such threats absorb the resources of the city, traumatize patients and staff, and inconvenience and terrorize a larger group. "For about five hours 47th Street became choked with emergency workers."

"If anthrax spores are inhaled, the bacteria they produce can cause death." At the office of Planned Parenthood in Kansas City, "only one employee, wearing gloves and a mask, opens the mail in an isolated room."

In November an administrative office of the United Methodist Church in Wichita, Kansas, received a letter threatening anthrax exposure. Also that month, eight abortion clinics in four Midwestern states, including one in Wichita, received similar letters, all hoaxes.

It is a sad fact that the FBI and the Department of Justice never took seriously the violence against clinics and doctors until the October 23, 1998, murder of Dr. Barnett Slepian.

It is also sad and even startling that the Catholic bishops and right-wing Protestant leaders, with an exception or two, have remained silent and have not urged their followers to respect the life of those with whom they disagree. The bishops' 27-page statement, "Living the Gospel of Life," in which they instructed American Catholics to put pressure on and vote only for anti-

Reprinted by permission from The Churchman/Human Quest, *July-August 1999.*

abortion politicians, was issued in November [1998], a month after Dr. Slepian was assassinated and well after others were killed. Warnings against such violence could easily have been included.

Right-wing columnist Cal Thomas blamed the killing of Dr. Slepian on the cheapening of life by legal abortion. He specifically blamed the "*New York Times* and other defenders of . . . abortion that contribute to the cheapening of life." (*Kansas City Star*, Nov. 30, 1998.)

This is now a familiar theme of the anti-abortion movement. Following the Kansas City anthrax scare at the Planned Parenthood clinic, the Western Region coordinator of Missouri Right to Life, in a viewpoint piece in the *Kansas City Star*, first expressed her "abhorrence of violence outside the abortion clinics." Then she launched into an attack on abortion, saying they wondered whether the violence "was set up by the abortion industry to look like the work of pro-life activists." Though she said she did not now believe that, she led readers to suppose it is plausible. She also said, "There is an axiom that violence begets violence," and referred to "the 36 million unborn babies destroyed by the violence of abortion."

Some religious groups believe that human beings exist at conception. The fertilized egg, however, is microscopic and weighs a fraction of an ounce, has no body, brain, or sex, which develops later. It does not implant in the uterus for some days after fertilization. There is no violence in a pill or other medical device that prevents implantation.

Millions of fertilized eggs are discarded by Nature or God and never implant. Up to 50 percent of those that implant are aborted naturally, but called miscarriages. Presumably abortion opponents do not claim God engages in violence or murder. Certainly Catholic theologians such as Augustine and Thomas Aquinas never assumed that a person or soul exists at conception.

Abortions after implantation are of two kinds: one is medically induced by a pill, and the other surgically induced, in each case with the request and consent of the woman. Most of us do not believe consensual medical or surgical action is violence.

Legally there are two types of abortion: elective and emergency. An elective abortion, which is chosen by the woman, must take place in the first trimester (within twelve weeks of pregnancy) or in the second trimester before viability. Physicians performing second trimester abortions must first determine that the fetus is too underdeveloped to survive outside the womb. After 24 weeks (the beginning of the third trimester) the procedure is not elective but emergency, in that the fetus is gravely or fatally impaired, or the woman's life or health is at risk. Ninety percent of abortions are performed in the first trimester, and 99 percent within 20 weeks or before viability.

Because the fetus feels no pain, a function of the brain as yet undeveloped, and the woman acts under her own will and conscience, it is still not violence to a human being.

It is the violent language such as "baby killer" that seems to motivate the violent wing of the right-to-life movement. However, an embryo or fetus is not yet a baby or child. This is a propaganda device known as *prolepsis*, which *Webster's Dictionary* defines as "describing an event as if it has already happened" when in fact it may be months away or never happen. An acorn, for example, is not yet an oak tree, and crushing an acorn is not the same as cutting down a 20 or 40-year-old tree.

It is not enough to say that abortion is not violent. Abortion is a positive decision and not a lesser evil. It gives women control over their lives, their fertility, their education, their vocations, and their responsibility to their families, and is therefore pro-family and pro-life. A book by Patricia Lunneborg, *Abortion: A Positive Decision,* confirms this in eleven chapters, one of which is "Abortion, Education and Careers."

The anti-abortion movement goes to great lengths to suggest that abortion is a psychological hazard, and urges women instead to give up unwanted children for adoption. Two recent studies demonstrate the fallacy of these ideas: A panel report published April 10, 1990, in the journal *Science* and commissioned by the American Psychological Association, was the result of research to determine if a valid conclusion could be drawn about post-abortion psychological effects. The panel surveyed more than 200 studies and found only about 19 or 20 that met solid scientific standards of investigations.

Their conclusion: "The weight of the evidence from scientific studies indicates that legal abortion of an unwanted pregnancy in the first trimester does not pose a psychological hazard for most women." The greatest distress it found "is likely to be before the abortion." The report also revealed that most women said they had feelings of relief and happiness after an abortion in the first trimester. (*New York Times,* April 6, 1990.)

On the other hand, mothers forced to give up their children for adoption have serious problems. The April 16, 1998, Westchester County, NY, *Reporter Dispatch* reported an historic Catholic mass in Buffalo, believed to be the first "Healing Mass." It was co-sponsored by the Diocese's Pro-Life Office and another group. The report said, "Mothers forced to give up their children not only suffer a sense of loss, but also guilt 'from not being able to tell your child you did not want to give him away. You need your child's forgiveness.'"

The conclusion is not only that abortion is a positive moral choice for an unwanted pregnancy but that it is essential for its defenders to broadcast its positive nature. It is a mistake to let those opposed to abortion create from unproven data the idea that abortion is immoral and violent. It is pro-life for the woman and her family, and demonstrates that American society cares about the health and welfare of women, who otherwise would be subject to compulsory pregnancy with all its risks, if this country again made abortion illegal.

THE POPE VERSUS THE BIBLE

The Vatican has begun a multimillion-dollar project that will strengthen its influence in the United States. After about ten years of planning, construction began this past September on what the July 23, 1997, *Washington Times* reported is a $50 million Pope John Paul II Cultural Center in Washington, D.C. The 100,000-square-foot center is being built next to the National Shrine of the Immaculate Conception and is being financed by a Detroit foundation.

The key to the purpose of this center is found in its focus on the teachings of the current pope and on such issues as abortion, birth control, euthanasia, assisted suicide, and ordination of women. It was described as "part interactive museum and part think tank." In other words, "it is intended to be akin to a presidential museum for the Pope" and also a right-wing propaganda agency to supplement the already Catholic-led Heritage Foundation, National Empowerment Television, and Free Congress Foundation. These have been promoting right-wing Vatican ideology in the American political sphere ever since Paul Weyrich, deacon in the Catholic Church, founded them and turned over the leadership of National Empowerment Television to William Bennett of the right-wing Catholic Campaign for America. Bennett is the former Secretary of Education under the Reagan administration and the nation's leading advocate of vouchers for private schools.

The *Washington Times* also reported that Detroit's Cardinal Adam Maida said the Pope wanted this memorial in Washington. It did not speculate about a Pope who would build such a memorial to himself instead of using such funds for efforts like eliminating poverty, war, disease, and other forms of injustice. As many progressive Catholics and others have long known, the Vatican is primarily a political and financial power institution functioning behind the pope's facade of spirituality.

This has been demonstrated particularly with the issues of abortion and birth control. When the Catholic bishops launched the right-wing religious movement in the United States with their Pastoral Plan for Pro-Life Activities on November 30, 1975, there was no right-wing religious consensus around which to unite. Abortion, including contraceptive birth control as the bishops defined it, became the major focus of both Catholic and Protestant right-wing groups. The use of contraceptives after intercourse to prevent implantation in the uterus was defined as abortion.

Reprinted by permission from The Humanist, *November/December 1997.*

Since there was no biblical basis for their position on abortion, the bishops relied exclusively on papal theology, using such phrases as "the sanctity of life from conception onwards" and "the church has a unique responsibility to transmit the teaching of Christ" with "regard to abortion" and "should show that abortion is a violation of God's laws."

In examining such statements and papal theology about abortion and birth control, it is essential to examine the biblical record. There is no reference in the Old or New Testament to the sacredness or sanctity of either human or fetal life. In fact, throughout the Bible people are murdered, slaughtered by the millions, sacrificed, beheaded, and crucified -- and, for a multitude of reasons, often at the instruction of or to appease God. This is especially true of the lack of sanctity of the fetus. In 2 Kings 15:16 there is reference to an order to smite all the people of a certain region "and all the women therein that were with child [are to be] ripped up." In Hosea 13:16 it says, "Their infants shall be dashed in pieces, and their women with child shall be ripped up."

When Isaiah seeks vengeance against Babylon, he asks God to see that "everyone that is found shall be thrust through . . . and they shall have no pity on the fruit of the womb; their eye shall not spare children" (Isaiah 13:15-18). The separate reference to children and fruit of the womb is to fetal life. These are not isolated references to violent abortion, as evident in Amos 2:9, Psalms 21:10, Deuteronomy 33:11, and elsewhere. There are also three leading biblical figures who wished for an abortion or miscarriage. Job (3:16) laments, "Why was I not as a hidden untimely birth, as infants that never see the light." Jeremiah (20:14-18) wishes he had been killed in his mother's womb. And Hosea (9:14) asked God "to give them a miscarrying womb and dry breasts."

Jesus, speaking of expected end time events, showed no special concern for fetal life: "Alas for those that are with child, and those that give suck in those days" (Matthew 24:19, Mark 13:11, and Luke 21:23). In Luke 23:29, he said the days are coming when they will say, "Blessed are the barren and wombs that never bore, and the breasts that never gave suck." There is actually one commandment from God to Moses to have a priest mix a potion that might produce an abortion if a man's wife has become pregnant by another man (Numbers 5:11-31).

None of the above passages affect the Vatican or its fundamentalist Protestant allies who are intent on using abortion and pro-life emphases as a way of getting theocratic control over the United States and women worldwide.

Moreover, the Vatican idea that human life begins with conception is an attempt to override the biblical idea that human life begins with breathing. The Hebrew word that describes a human being is *nephesh* -- the breathing one. It occurs 775 times in the Hebrew Bible. It is obvious that in Hebrew thought a fetus is not a living human being because it does not breathe on its own.

Pro-life groups mistakenly apply one of the Ten Commandments -- "You shall not kill" -- to a fetus. That commandment did not refer to animals, as Israelites killed to eat and to sacrifice. It did not apply to their enemies in war, and it did not even apply to all Israelites because anyone who cursed his or her father or mother was to be killed (Exodus 21:17). It is desperation that makes "pro-lifers" apply the commandment to an embryo or fetus because there is no explicit reference in the entire Bible that is anti-abortion or pro-life with respect to a fetus.

The fact that the Catholic bishops are using abortion to control America is evident in the following excerpt from an article in the August 29, 1997, *National Catholic Reporter* discussing women who became pregnant by priests:

> Some priest-fathers are willing to become involved with, if not willing
> to fully acknowledge, their offspring. But sadly, others simply arrange
> abortions, sometimes with the acknowledgement of their bishops.

If one examines Vatican dogma, it is only fetuses that have a "right to life." The pregnant woman whose life or health is endangered by the fetus has no right to life. Over the centuries, the Vatican has been involved in the direct or indirect slaughter of millions of people, including the enemies in the Crusades; the heretics and Jews in the Holy Inquisition; Protestants in the religious wars in Europe; Moors driven out of Spain; Muslims driven out of Eastern Europe by Polish-led armies; Jews, gypsies, and communists in World War II; and both Orthodox and Muslim Serbs killed by the Croatian Ustashi Catholics during the 1930s and 1940s.

If it is argued by the pro-life movement that the Vatican has changed in recent years, it is only necessary to note that, since 1975 when the bishops wrote their pro-life pastoral, the Vatican has been involved with its Maronite militia in Lebanon and the thousands of murders of suspected communists and political dissidents in Argentina described by Emilio F. Mignone, a Roman Catholic, in his book *Witness to Truth: The Complicity of Church and Dictatorship in Argentina*.

Moreover, to show his devotion to "life," Pope John Paul II on April 21, 1986, raised the twenty-nine military vicariates around the world to the status of dioceses. These have military jurisdiction and are governed by prelates with the same rights and privileges as a bishop. It was the military vicars in Argentina who gave the Church's approval for the military coup of March 24,

1976, which led to the murders in the subsequent "Dirty War" in that country. There are at least twelve such vicariates in the Americas (including the United States), nine in Europe, three in Asia, three in Africa, and two in Oceania. The pope also insisted -- against the initial vote of the U.S. bishops -- on maintaining the right to use nuclear weapons by preserving the doctrine of deterrence.

It is thus obvious that the term *pro-life* refers only to embryos and fetuses and not to living human beings who incur the ill will of the Vatican from time to time. That is why the Vatican has institutionalized militarism within its own organization. It also goes to great lengths to prevent individual countries, as well as the United Nations, from saving the health and lives of women through family planning, birth control, and legalized abortion.

In the United States, the Vatican has convinced the Christian Coalition, Focus on the Family, the Mormons, the Southern Baptist Convention, and other Protestants to abandon biblical principles and accept papal theology. Together these groups have prevailed upon the Republican Party to write Vatican theology into the party platform as follows: "The unborn child has a fundamental right to life that cannot be infringed." This means that men and fetuses have a right to life at all times, but women lose that right when they become pregnant.

The Vatican has tremendous influence on many governments, on the military, on Congress, and on many Protestants. It is primarily the civil or ecclesiastical disobedience of progressive Catholics that keeps it from much greater political control over the lives of women and people generally. It is crucial that Vatican theology, ideology, and power be scrutinized, analyzed, and publicly opposed if essential freedoms are to be preserved.

ROME'S SEXUAL RULES FOR US ALL?

The Vatican, in its preoccupation with sexual issues, has announced its opposition to at least fourteen current medical technologies, among them artificial insemination, efforts to secure the birth of a baby without sexual intercourse, and prenatal diagnosis, including the use of amniocentesis and ultrasonic techniques if they may lead to abortion of malformed fetuses.

The Vatican statement, "Instruction on Respect for Human Life in Its Origin and on the Dignity of Procreation," is rooted in its idea of nature, that "the transmission of human life is entrusted by nature to a personal and conscious act and as such is subject to the all-holy laws of God: immutable and inviolable laws which must be recognized and observed."

An orthodox rabbi, Dr. Moses Tendler, who teaches ethics at Yeshiva University, has said, "The word 'natural' is a holy word to the Pope and 'unnatural' means evil." Jewish understanding is different: "To us 'unnatural' is a mitzvah," which means a virtuous deed. "Unnatural is not a sin but an opportunity to complete God's work." Dr. Tendler said Jewish law endorses artificial insemination as well as *in vitro* fertilization when the husband's sperm and wife's egg are involved and in some cases would permit the use of sperm from a third party. He added: "You cannot commit adultery with a catheter or a hypodermic syringe."

The Vatican, however, insists that for "a truly responsible procreation . . . the unborn child must be the fruit of marriage" and that "fertilization of a married woman with the sperm of a donor different from her husband and fertilization with the husband's sperm of an ovum not coming from his wife are morally illicit." The Vatican justifies this position with assertions for which there is no evidence, including such statements as "artificial fertilization is contrary to the unity of marriage, to the dignity of the spouses" and "damage to the personal relationships within the family has repercussions on civil society. . . . " Then, from such untrue generalizations, the "Instruction" takes a great leap in asserting that "what threatens the unity and stability of the family is a source of dissension, disorder and injustice in the whole of social life." Actually, it could be said that Vatican insistence on controlling the sexual decisions of families is the source of dissension. Professor Daniel Maguire, a Catholic theologian, put it: "The Vatican is squandering its moral authority on issues where it has no privileged knowledge or expertise."

Reprinted by permission from The Churchman/Human Quest, *June-July, 1987.*

The Vatican document specifically condemns the collection of sperm through masturbation but permits "medical intervention . . . when it seeks to assist the conjugal act either in order to facilitate its performance or in order to enable it to achieve its objective once it has been normally performed." This is not spelled out. However, one medical ethics consultant for Catholic hospitals, Father John Connery, explains: "If a couple, let's say, had intercourse and the doctor then took a syringe and went into the vagina and got the sperm and then injected it farther into the uterus or the fallopian tube -- if that could be done, I think you could justify it." The doctor, in other words, could wait outside the bedroom until invited in with a syringe in hand to be thrust into the vagina. How is that for preserving "the dignity of the spouses," Vatican style?

Still other Catholic medical authorities said sperm "could be obtained ethically by using a condom pierced with holes to allow some sperm to escape." Such a condom might be acceptable, though one without holes would not be, as it is a means of contraception. Church authorities seem not to have learned that Vatican legalism requires permissible absurdities as the price of appearing to be moral.

The Holy See acknowledges that "the desire for a child is natural" and especially "if the couple is affected by sterility which seems incurable. Nevertheless, marriage does not confer upon the spouses the right to have a child, but only the right to perform those natural acts which are *per se* ordered to creation." The Vatican is opposed to *in vitro* fertilization (in a dish or test tube) or to any other reproduction unless it comes from "the mutual self-giving of the spouses, of their love and of their fidelity." A letter to the editor of the *Kansas City Star* included this: "If love is the buzzword here, then why is abortion not sanctioned when conception results from rape or incest? Or why not birth control when sex is purely sex and no love or commitment exists? At least, when science produces life you can be reasonably sure it is done in the name of love and want."

The Vatican "Instruction," however, repeats its previous positions, stating that "contraception deliberately deprives the conjugal act of its openness to procreation and in this way brings about a voluntary dissociation of the ends of marriage," and "human life must be absolutely respected and protected from the moment of conception." The "Instruction" makes an absolute statement about conception that "from the first instant, the programme is fixed as to what this living being will be. . . . " In other words, we are determined biologically without regard to any interaction with the environment of the mother's womb including drugs, alcohol, nicotine she may be ingesting, malnutrition from her poverty, damage from illness, tension or harm from subsequent rape, or repeated wife abuse, etc.

The "Instruction," while certain of human biological characteristics at conception, nevertheless says: "The Magisterium has not expressly committed itself to an affirmation of a philosophical nature" at conception with respect to the human person or "spiritual soul."

Prenatal diagnosis is acceptable if it "makes it possible to anticipate earlier and more effectively certain therapeutic medical or surgical procedures." It is not permissible if "it is done with the thought of possibly inducing an abortion depending upon the results: a diagnosis which shows the existence of a malformation or a hereditary disease must not be the equivalent of a death sentence." In other words, a fetus with a disease that will lead to a prolonged painful death a few years after birth must not be aborted. The Vatican thus ignores such cruelty to children in its dogmatic commitment against abortion.

The Vatican speaks of the embryo or fetus as "an innocent human being." "Innocent" has at least two meanings. It comes from the Latin word, *noceo*, which means "harm" and the prefix *in*, which means "not." But one cannot say that every fetus or every birth is not harmful or dangerous to the mother either physically or emotionally, as in the case of rape or incest. Another meaning of "innocent" is that it is free from original sin or free from any tendency to put its own interests ahead of mother, father, siblings, and society. In the interest of dogma, Vatican theology is found wanting. Or else the Vatican by implication recognizes that characteristics of human personhood such as self-centeredness and the ability to choose evil over good do not exist until after birth.

The "Instruction" condemns absolutely *in vitro* fertilization and embryo transfer, even "when there is no other way of overcoming the sterility which is a source of suffering . . . " because "the generation of the human person" is not the "result and fruit of a conjugal act. . . . " In other words, *in vitro* fertilization "establishes the domination of technology over the origin and destiny of the human person." At several points the "Instruction" gives rights to a fetus that does not yet exist. For example, it asserts "the child's right to be conceived and brought into the world in marriage."

The chief criticism which must be leveled against this "Instruction" is the Vatican's demand that Catholic sexual ethics be legislated so that everyone has to be ruled by Vatican dogma. The following demonstrate the Vatican's effort to control the sex life of non-Catholics by law. "Politicians must commit themselves, through this intervention upon public opinion, to securing the widest possible consensus on such essential points. . . . " They are expected to enact into law "appropriate penal sanctions" for any abortion, for artificial procreation, artificial insemination using the sperm of a third party, embryo banks, post mortem insemination, and "surrogate motherhood."

The Vatican further asserts that there is a fundamental "right to life and physical integrity from the moment of conception" which "must be recognized and respected by civil society and the political authority" and "the child's right to be conceived, brought into the world and brought up by his parents." For the first time in such a document, Catholic politicians must be responsive to papal sexual teaching and Catholic laity are expected to influence non-Catholic politicians to legislate the same teaching. Many church members will not agree with part or all of this "Instruction."

Trisha Flynn, a Scripps Howard columnist and "a practicing Catholic," wrote in the April 3, 1987, *Seattle Times*: "The idea of a bunch of celibate old men sitting around the Vatican discussing pregnancy is beyond me."

In the U.S., another group of celibate old men will seek to write this into American law. These men, who have already mobilized the resources of their church to fight abortion and contraception, are now expected to send those same forces into battle to impose more far ranging sexual rules on the general population.

POPE ASKS DISOBEDIENCE TO U.S. LAW

Pope John Paul II on March 25, 1995, promulgated his papal encyclical, *"Evangelium Vitae"* requiring the obedience of Roman Catholics in opposing abortion and euthanasia when they vote or have anything to do with legitimizing those issues. The encyclical is therefore an explicit instruction to obedient Catholics in Congress, state legislators and even to Supreme Court justices in their official capacity to oppose any law or proposed law which would permit abortion.

The following are the crucial sentences in a much longer papal decree:

> No circumstances, no purpose, no law whatsoever can ever make licit an act which is intrinsically illicit, since it is contrary to the Law of God which is written in every heart, knowable by reason itself, and proclaimed by the church.
>
> Abortion and euthanasia are thus crimes which no human law can claim to legitimize. There is no obligation in conscience to obey such laws; instead there is a grave and clear obligation to oppose them by conscientious objection.
>
> In the case of an intrinsically unjust law, such as a law permitting abortion or euthanasia, it is never licit to obey it, or to "take part in a propaganda campaign in favour of such a law, *or vote for it.*" (emphasis supplied)

The Pope also insisted that his authority to interpret what is moral must be placed ahead of democratic judgments of people whose interpretation of the will of God differs from his. He specifically stated, "Democracy cannot be idolized to the point of making it a substitute for morality." He also said, "As a result we have what appear to be dramatically opposed tendencies."

It is not unusual for absolute monarchs to assert their judgments as superior to the will of the people. But in a religiously diverse society such as the United States there are those who do not want their legislators, presidents, governors and judges to obey the Pope rather than take seriously the constitutional oath to obey the Constitution and the will of the people.

At the same time this writer acknowledges that the Pope has a right to issue any encyclical he wants, even though he is the head of a foreign state and a citizen of Poland. His decrees, however, need careful examination

---

Reprinted by permission from The Churchman/Human Quest, *March-April 1996.*

when they are applied to laws that were enacted by and apply to Roman Catholics as well as to non-Catholics in the United States.

For example, the Pope is clearly wrong in asserting that abortion "is contrary to the Law of God." There is no statement in the New Testament which validates the papal position. Moreover, his interpretation of "the Law of God" is not "written in every heart, knowable by reason itself" or it would be accepted by other churches and faiths as well as the non-religious.

When the Pope speaks out of conscience he is right in saying that conscience may cause some people to violate a particular law. But conscience may also support laws which give women the right to choose ending an early pregnancy. The Pope has never acknowledged that the lives and health of women are important enough to permit them to terminate a pregnancy which endangers them or their families.

The Pope is also clearly wrong in telling American Catholics who have been elected or appointed to public office that they must obey him. If such officials were to acknowledge that he determines how they should vote, there would be no point in democratic elections even in heavily Catholic areas. Many if not most Catholics do not automatically vote the way their bishops or the pope want.

The Pope is also wrong in defining contraceptives that function after "sperm unites with egg" as abortion. Conception is not complete or viable until the fertilized egg is implanted in the uterus, which generally occurs about ten days to two weeks after ovulation. Yet he condemns contraceptives because they "really act as abortifacients in the very early stages of the development of the life of the new human being." . . .

Certainly this papal encyclical is a crucial threat to American democracy and to a rule of law. Yet the press, including the progressive Catholic press, has paid it little if any attention. Did our readers know about this encyclical before reading this article?

WHOSE PERSONAL CONSCIENCE?

Recently a man I have never met and whose religion I do not know sent me a copy of a speech by Pope John Paul II that I did not know existed. It is his address to U.S. bishops at their *ad limina* visit to the Vatican June 27, 1998. *Ad limina* is Latin for "to the highest authority," which means a visit to the one person who believes he is chosen to speak for Jesus Christ on earth. My correspondent, who asked me to comment on it, evidently assumed my comment would be critical because the Pope was clearly trying to discredit American democracy and freedom of conscience in an effort to get papal doctrine accepted in the United States.

Although the pope is making the case against self-government and individual freedom to choose between good and evil, he is really claiming that only the Church and he as the Vicar of Christ know the truth and must prevail in government. He said, "The notion of freedom and personal autonomy is superficially attractive; endorsed by intellectuals, the media, legislature and the courts. . . . Yet it ultimately destroys the personal good of individuals and the common good of society."

The Pope then asserts that the "nobility of men and women lies not simply in the capacity to choose but in the capacity to choose wisely" which means "witnessing to the moral laws inscribed in the human heart." He claims that the Church promotes "essential truths"; therefore, "the good of the person lies in *being* in the Truth and *doing* the Truth."

The Pope then directly involves himself in American politics by saying: "When the Church teaches, for example, that abortion, sterilization or euthanasia are always inadmissible, she is giving expression to the universal moral law inscribed on the human heart, and is therefore teaching something which is binding on everyone's conscience."

The Pope is of course in error in speaking about the "universal moral law," since abortion were widely performed in the ancient world and were never mentioned by Jesus or the apostles. In fact, there are three instances in the Old Testament where someone wished for abortion or death in the womb. Job laments (3:16) "why was I not as a hidden untimely birth, as infants that never see the light?" Jeremiah (20:14-18) wishes he had been killed in his mother's womb," and Hosea (9:14) asked God to "give them a miscarrying womb and dry breasts."

In Hosea 13:16 it says, "Their infants shall be dashed to pieces and their

Reprinted by permission from The Churchman/Human Quest, *November-December 1999.*

women with child shall be ripped up.'" In another passage Isaiah (13:15-18) asks God to see that ""everyone that is found shall they thrust through . . . and they shall have no pity on the fruit of the womb; their eye shall not spare children." There are other similar references in the Hebrew scriptures.

Even the early Catholic theologians such as Augustine and Thomas Aquinas did not condemn abortion by what is defined by the Pope as abortion: any termination of life after conception. Until 1869 with the issuance of a papal encyclical, most Catholic theologians did not oppose abortion within at least 40 days after the start of pregnancy, and did not think of it as the taking of human life.

Therefore this Pope is falsifying scriptural and theological history and doctrine in speaking of "the universal moral law inscribed on the human heart," and of abortion as "always morally inadmissible." It is no virtue to claim "truth" for such papal error. Yet this is what the Pope claims in his statement that he and the bishops "are defending and promoting not arbitrary claims made by the Church but essential truths and therefore the good of individuals and the common good of society."

The Pope arrives at his position by defining "freedom" not in terms of free will or democracy, but the "right to do what I ought to do, to adhere freely to what is good and true," which, it is implied, is found only in the Pope's truth.

Then the Pope proceeds to redefine conscience not as something that individuals have "to determine what constitutes good and evil," but as something that must "correspond to the 'eternal, objective and universal divine law.'" He said, "As bishops you have to teach that freedom of conscience is never freedom from the truth but always and only freedom in the truth." Throughout this speech it is the Church that has "the Truth."

Amazingly, the Pope said, "Respect for the rights of conscience is deeply ingrained in your national culture, which was formed in part by emigrants who came to the New World to vindicate their religious and moral convictions in the face of persecution." This is amazing because the persecution was that of the Catholic Church and other theocracies, which the Vatican is now trying to reinstate through political enforcement of its position on abortion and other sex-related policies.

Nevertheless, the Pope went on to tell the bishops, "American society's historic admiration for men and women of conscience is the ground on which you can teach the truth about conscience today."

The Pope's attempt to define conscience as agreement with papal dogma is at odds with both the secular and religious understanding in America. A conscientious objector to war as defined by the Supreme Court does not have to belong to a pacifist church; Catholics whose conscience is against all wars are valid objectors when they reject the Church's position about just wars. And non-religious objectors also have a conscience that is recognized.

Episcopal Bishop George Leslie Cadigan articulated in 1971 the usual American understanding of conscience, which stands in contrast to the papal or Vatican definition of conscience. Speaking about abortion, Bishop Cadigan said,

> It is at once the glory and the burden of each of us that we are called upon to make such difficult personal decisions according to our consciences. When we deny that liberty to anyone of our number, we give away a part of our own birthright. When, more specifically, we condemn a woman for making an independent judgment according to her own conscience relating to her reproductive life, we denigrate her personhood.
>
> The "rightness" or "wrongness" of abortion as the solution of a problem pregnancy is not the critical issue here. The issue is the larger ethical one: can any one of us stand in the role of judge for the personal decisions of others? What robes shall we wear? Greater than the debatable immorality of terminating an undesired pregnancy is the immorality of refusing a woman access to medical help when she has determined that she needs it.

Finally, the Pope engages in enormous hypocrisy. It is the Vatican and Catholic bishops that are deeply involved in a political "Right to [fetal] Life" campaign that dominates and divides the United States politically. Yet the Pope said to the American bishops, "It should be clear that the Church addresses issues of public life not for political reasons, but as a servant of the truth about the human person . . . " And, he added, "It is a tribute to the Church and to the openness of American society that so many Catholics in the United States are involved in political life." He goes on to say that if American "constitutional and statutory law are not held accountable to the objective [papal] moral law," then "democratic politics is reduced to a raw contest for power."

It is ironic that, in the sexual politics of the Vatican, the description is apt; there is indeed a "raw contest for power."

Everything in the Pope's idea of truth and morality hinges on his definition of truth: "In proclaiming the truth that God has given men and women an inestimable and inalienable right from the moment of conception, you are helping to rebuild the moral foundations for a genuine culture."

Not once in this or any other of his political speeches has this pope condemned the killing of physicians or deplored the deaths of women who would suffer if they were never allowed life-saving abortion. In the name of life he winks at the culture of death that flows from his position.

If we look again at the papal statement that the Church is merely "giving expression to the universal moral law inscribed in the human heart . . . ," we must note that it is human beings who have had to oppose church and state for the right to reproductive freedom.

The countries that did not have to oppose the Vatican were the earliest to adopt the moral value and legal right of abortion. In colonial and early America there were no laws against abortion prior to 1821 in Connecticut, 1827 in Illinois, and 1830 in New York. Czechoslovakia allowed it in 1920 and restricted it in 1936; Iceland allowed it in 1935; Sweden in 1939; Denmark in 1939. By 1960 Poland, Czechoslovakia, Bulgaria, Romania and Yugoslavia specifically legalized it, as did China in 1957, Finland in 1951, Norway in 1965 (later rescinded), Holland in 1967; England in 1967. In 1963 in England, a report entitled "Towards a Quaker View of Sex" states unequivocally: "We reject almost completely the traditional approach of the organized church to morality with its supposition that it knows what is right and wrong."

In France in 1975 abortion on request was legislated for the first ten weeks of pregnancy. This was the first largely Catholic country to legalize it. East Germany in 1972 was followed by West Germany in 1976. Italy in May 1978 approved abortion on request despite the Vatican and the Vatican-controlled Christian Democratic Party. Austria, Singapore, and Tunisia have abortion by request.

In Africa, Kenya, Ghana, Tanzania, Zambia, Zimbabwe, Gambia, Uganda and Sierra Leone have legalized abortion.

Legal abortion varies from country to country. In some there are various restrictions and in some there is abortion on request. However, the point in this brief survey is to demonstrate that the papacy is engaged in misleading rhetoric when the Pope says that the Church "is giving expression to the universal moral law inscribed in the human heart and is therefore teaching something which is binding on everyone's conscience."

This recent effort by the Pope to have an influence in American politics is not the first. It is part of a long series of efforts to achieve what would in effect be theocratic dominance in American life. That, however, is the subject of another article.

In summarizing the papal address it is essential to note that Pope John Paul has redefined freedom from its usual meaning to agreement with or obedience to whatever Truth is set forth by the Vatican. Conscience has also been redefined to mean obedience to institutional Truth.

This is itself a conformity to Catholic tradition that goes back at least to the Inquisition. In the Vatican today what used to be called "The Holy Office of the Roman and Universal Inquisition" has a gentler name: "The Congregation for the Doctrine of the Faith."

Hans Küng, arguably Europe's most prominent Catholic theologian, noted that the head of that Congregation, Cardinal Ratzinger, travels "to the relevant country to make unequivocally clear what the 'Catholic truth' is." He wrote: "No one is burned at the stake anymore, but careers and psyches are destroyed as required." Küng was forbidden to teach in a Catholic university.

With respect to the United States, a prominent Catholic theologian, Rev. Charles Curran, was dismissed from teaching at the Catholic University in Washington because he did not follow the Vatican "Truth" on such reproductive issues as contraceptive birth control and abortion. He has since taught at Southern Methodist University. Others have similarly been dismissed in the United States and other countries because their understanding of freedom and conscience differed from papal Truth.

So when the Pope uses the phrase "universal moral truth" it is essential to understand that it is not really universal and not necessarily moral, but his way of expecting absolute loyalty to an authoritarian institution whose Truth is what the Pope says it is.

What is profoundly disturbing is that the Vatican is intent on renewing the medieval idea that Christendom not only exists, but that it is ruled from one source and by one man, who has a tragically limited understanding of morality, human rights, scientific fact and respect for others' views.

THE TWO FACES OF MR. HYDE

Their bold attack through the impeachment process on a president who has refused to accept abortion politics promoted by far-right Catholics and Protestants, and who has defended separation of church and state, is simply one evidence that the fanatical religious right will stop at nothing. For example, all of the twenty-one Republicans on the Judiciary Committee voted to stop payment of the United States' debt of about $1.5 billion to the United Nations by amending the appropriation bill so that it would ban international nongovernmental organizations "from lobbying foreign governments on abortion laws, even with their own money." This, continued the *New York Times* of September 24, 1998, "would require non-governmental organizations to silence themselves in legitimate political debate over reproductive rights in their own countries." The same editorial says, "Few international organizations that seek population aid from the United States perform abortions" but this right-wing rule "would prohibit these groups from sponsoring workshops on abortion issues, distributing materials, or making public statements that call attention to defects in a country's abortion laws."

Although the *Times* never mentions the Vatican, the background of this effort to silence free speech and lobbying in other countries is the failure of the Vatican to prevent outspoken support for reproductive freedom for women in many countries. In heavily Catholic countries in Europe, abortion has been legalized: in France in 1975; in Austria and in Italy, the home of the Vatican, in 1978.

The Pope and the Italian hierarchy went all out to prevent legal abortion in Italy but, after the fall of the Vatican-influenced government over the issue of abortion led by thousands of Italian women, the new government voted for free state subsidies for abortion-on-demand in the first ninety days of pregnancy for any woman over age eighteen who said childbirth would endanger her physical or mental health.

The only hope for silencing advocates of reproductive freedom overseas therefore lies with the U.S. religious right, led by the persistent right-wing Catholic, Christopher Smith, a New Jersey Republican who for years has pressed this issue in the House.

The most persistent Vatican loyalist in Congress, however, is Henry Hyde. Immediately after the U.S. Catholic bishops launched their campaign against abortion in 1975, Hyde led their campaign in Congress. When the

Reprinted by permission from The Humanist, *January/February 1999.*

Labor-Health, Education, and Welfare appropriation bill for fiscal year 1976-1977 was considered in the House, Hyde inserted the following amendment: "None of the funds appropriated under this Act shall be used to pay for abortions or to promote or encourage abortion."

Waldo Zimmerman, a Roman Catholic, in his book *Condemned to Live: The Plight of the Unwanted Child,* writes:

> Congressman Hyde, who is a devout Catholic, tried to discount the religious angle. He said, "The old argument that we who oppose abortions are trying to impose our religious concepts on other people is totaly absurd.Theology does not animate me; biology does." . . . No one who is familiar with the situation will take Brother Hyde at face value. It is obvious that he and his colleagues were following the blueprint for political action prepared by the Roman hierarchy's Pastoral Plan for Pro-Life Activities announced only a few months previously. . . .
>
> Colleagues paint Congressman Hyde in glowing terms: a fine character, a genial, friendly compassionate man . . . a virtual prototype of the legendary Dr. Jekyll. It is only when the subject of family planning comes up that he begins to change. At the drop of a word--abortion--there is a metamorphosis as strange as that in [Robert Louis] Stevenson's masterpiece; the genial Dr. Jekyll becomes the monstrous Mr. Hyde. The Congressman bares his fangs, throws compassion to the winds, scoffs at the countless lives wrecked by his heartless amendment and condemns thousands of *unwanted children* to a miserable unwanted life.

When the Senate objected to the Hyde language in the 1976-1977 appropriation bill, conferees from the Senate and House met to resolve differences. Seven of the eleven House conferees were Catholics and not one woman was on the House committee. As a result, a deadlock in the committee lasted an unusual five months. It was resolved finally with a compromise motion advanced by House Republican leader Robert Michel, which the House accepted by a vote of 181 to 167.

The question of the constitutionality of the Hyde amendment was brought before Federal Judge John F. Dooling in the Eastern District of New York. Dooling is a practicing Catholic who took thirteen months to hear the evidence. In his 428-page decision that struck down the Hyde amendment, the judge says the amendment reflects a sectarian position that "is not genuinely argued; it is adamantly asserted." He concludes that Hyde's amendment is religiously motivated legislation with a specific theological viewpoint that violates dissenters' First Amendment rights.

Dooling's ruling was later overturned by the U.S. Supreme Court on another ground--that states are not required to pay for abortion. Supreme Court Justice William Brennan, a Catholic not in the service of the Vatican, writes about the Hyde amendment:

> Both by design and in effect it serves to coerce indigent pregnant women to bear children that they would not otherwise elect to have. By funding all expenses associated with childbirth and none of the expenses incurred in terminating pregnancy, the government literally makes an offer that the indigent woman cannot afford to refuse.

Hyde's religious bias is also evident in his actions as chair of the Republican Platform Committee, which again and again has inserted into the party's platform this statement: "The unborn child has a fundamental right to life that cannot be infringed." This clearly means that men and fetuses have a fundamental right to life but pregnant women do not. In 1996, Hyde loaded the Platform Committee with anti-abortionists so that the presidential candidate, Bob Dole, could not control it. Dole wanted some statement that would express tolerance for pro-choice Republicans, but Hyde did not yield on that point.

In an open letter, Hyde invited Catholics to help him develop the party's 1996 platform. He wrote: "Catholics are a powerful voice of moral authority and fulfill a growing leadership role in the Republican Party." More than any other politician or member of Congress, Hyde has steadily tried to identify the Republican Party with right-wing Vatican issues. He also says in that letter, "as a Catholic, I believe the basic principles of Catholic teaching are ideologically, philosophically, and morally aligned with the Republican Party."

Hyde rigidly follows the Vatican position not only against family planning but against separation of church and state. In November 1996, he introduced a religious equality amendment to the Constitution that would end separation of church and state and permit government funding of religion. It reads:

> Neither the United States nor any state shall deny benefits to or otherwise discriminate against any private person or group on account of religious expression, belief, or identity; nor shall the prohibition on laws respecting an establishment of religion be construed to require such discrimination.

Hyde decided to attach this to the Prayer Amendment of Protestant fundamentalist Ernest Istook so that the phrase "deny equal access to a benefit on account of religion" would be accepted as well as pubulic school prayer.

All of these Hyde positions are relevant to the impeachment process because Bill Clinton is the first president since Hyde was elected in 1974 who, by his leadership and vetoes, has defended family planning, abortion rights, and the separation of church and state. In other words, over the last few years Clinton has been the chief obstacle to the Vatican's efforts on these issues and hence has become an enemy of Hyde and the Vatican.

In September 1998, I received information from New York attorney John Tomasin, whose religious persuasion, if any, I do not know. He wrote to others as well, suggesting that "Henry Hyde recuse himself as Chairman of the House Judiciary Committee to insure a fair, impartial and unbiased preliminary impeachment inquiry." Tomasin included two supporting documents issued by Pope John Paul II that would require Hyde's obedience.

The first document is *Evangelium Vitae*, issued in 1995, which forbids faithful Catholics with respect to "a law permitting abortion" ever "to obey it, or to take part in a propaganda campaign in favor of such a law, or vote for it." The second document, *Ad Tuendam Fidem*, issued in May 1998, is an incorporation into canon law that requires obedience to the pope by all Christians on such doctrines as abortion. It specifically says, "All Christian faithful are therefore bound to avoid contrary doctrines. . . . Therefore anyone who rejects propositions which are to be held definitively, sets himself against the teaching of the Catholic Church." In comment on these papal doctrines, Tomasin states:

> It is well known that President Clinton is pro-choice and has recently vetoed anti-abortion legislation, and is considered the major obstacle to laws limiting or prohibiting abortion. The faithful are duty bound by the Pope to oppose him, and to remove him as such obstacle, if at all possible.

Henry Hyde even aligns himself with Joseph Scheidler, who was convicted of playing a role in coordinated assaults on abortion clinics. The *Wanderer* of October 5, 1998, reports that, during a trial brought by the National Organization for Women against Scheidler, Hyde said on the witness stand, "I cannot imagine a situation in which I would not want to be associated with Joe Scheidler."

Scheidler refuses to condemn anti-choice violence and had a key part in the founding of Operation Rescue, a violent wing of the anti-abortion movement. He is also a cofounder of the Pro-Life Action Network, which the

Wanderer of February 27, 1992, describes as "a deliberately loose-knit network which meets annually to plan strategies for coordinated assaults on abortion clinics or pro-choice politicians and which subsequently gave rise to Operation Rescue."

Scheidler was even arrested for disrupting an inaugural mass for pro-choice Republican Governor Pete Wilson of California, according to United Press International on January 30, 1991. and on July 16, 1992, the *Wanderer* reports that Scheidler claims credit for devising a "well-organized carefully planned effort" to hound Clinton "at every whistle stop and every coffee klatch" during that year's presidential campaign.

If there is any doubt about Hyde's enmity to Clinton it was evident in Hyde's burst of temper when he accused the White House of revealing his extramarital affair and demanded an FBI investigation. Rabbi Mark Levin, in the *Kansas City Star* of October 1998, says, "The FBI is a powerful tool. Charges of impeachment were threatened against President Nixon for misuse of his power to use the FBI to investigate individuals. Let us not again walk that path of FBI investigations to control perceived political enemies and chill political debate."

Although Henry Hyde is the right-wing Vatican point man in Congress, he is not an isolated individual leader. A monumental book--*Papal Power: A Study of Vatican Control Over Lay Catholic Elites,* written by Jean-Guy Vaillancourt, a Catholic professor at the University of Montreal--describes the Vatican's organization and use of key laypeople to promote the church's political and economic power. That carefully documented study of papal control of lay elites in Europe, chiefly Italy, has its parallel in the United States. Certain key laypeople--such as William Bennett, the chief advocate of vouchers for religious schools; Paul Weyrich, the founder of the right-wing Heritage Foundation and the Free Congress Foundation; Henry Hyde and Christopher Smith in Congress; and many others--serve as apparently secular advocates or "front" people for important church interests and obscure the behind-the-scenes influence of the Vatican and members of the hierarchy, such as Cardinal John O'Connor.

There is in the Vatican a highly secret Pontifical Council for the Laity, which is not an organization of laity but is tightly controlled, according to Vaillancourt, "through the inclusion of more cardinals, bishops and priests in the leadership positions of that organization." This means that key Catholic politicians in the United States who are responsive to the cardinals and bishops do not ever identify themselves as representing the political and economic interests of the Vatican. In turn, the institution supports these right-wing leaders and their political postions by turning many churches into an essentially Catholic political party.

In his book *Condemned to Live*, Waldo Zimmerman describes this coordinated support as follows:

> The "secret weapon" in the anti-abortionists' arsenal is the millions of children in Catholic schools, their "shock troops" for staging massive demonstrations and letter-writing campaigns. Every year parochial school children look forward eagerly to January 22, when thousands of them will be treated to a free trip to Washington and other metropolitan centers for demonstrations marking the anniversary of the Supreme Court's 1973 decision on abortion. There were as many as a thousand or two--often more--in similar demonstrations throughout the country. . . .
>
> The January marches on Washington are staged predominantly by elementary and high school students carrying rosaries and miniature statues of the Virgin Mary. . . . Distributed at the masses are letters and bulletins thoroughly informing parishioners about specific bills, telling them how to compose a letter to congressmen or state legislators and exactly what to write. School children are offered free time and other inducements for writing such letters.

In essence, the Vatican and its representatives in the United States are advocating a theocracy, which has been repudiated by Catholics in Europe. Unless liberal Catholics, Jews, Protestants, humanists, and others organize to oppose such theocratic action, what appears simply to be right-wing politics will be even more subversive of democracy.

THE RUN OF WHOSE LIFE?

Randall Terry, a fundamentalist Protestant and the [former] leader of Operation Rescue, one of the anti-abortion movement's most violent organizations, is running for Congress against incumbent Maurice Hinchey, a Democrat in New York's twenty-sixth district. Terry views his candidacy as "a natural referendum on abortion and homosexuality because anti-life and anti-family groups across America will support Representative Hinchey." However, Terry's candidacy is also a referendum on his advocacy of violence and death, and if he gets the support he expects from so-called pro-life groups, they expose themselves to the charge of being pro-death.

Terry has been a staunch advocate of assassinating medical personnel involved in abortion clinics. In 1989, he and his followers gathered in front of Boulder, Colorado, physician Warren M. Hern's office and prayed for the doctor's execution. In 1993, following the assassination of Florida doctor David Gunn, Terry again broadcast a call for Hern's murder.

Even so, in a letter in the January 5, 1998, issue of the far-right Catholic periodical the *Wanderer,* Terry speaks of his opponent as a "hard core pro-death leader in Congress" and a "leader of a growing number of treacherous politicians who support special rights for the militant sodomites." He uses such extremist language because he claims, "Hinchey wants to use our tax money to promote homosexuality to the teenage generation" and speaks of "Hinchey's support of forced abortion in Red China."

In his appeal to readers of the *Wanderer* for funds to begin his advertising attacks on Hinchey, Terry actually used his Operation Rescue as a campaign ploy. He wrote:

> I don't just talk about what I'm going to do; I do it. For example, in 1988 when I launched Operation Rescue, I said I would lead tens of thousands of Christians to the abortion mills to save babies from abortion. . . . By God's grace I did it. The results were hundreds of rescue missions that saved thousands of babies who otherwise would have been killed.

There is no evidence that Terry or his groups intimidated enough women to prevent that many abortions. There is evidence, however, that Terry intimidates doctors. In her March 15, 1993, column, Ellen Goodman wrote:

Reprinted by permission from The Humanist, *May/June 1998.*

Anyone who wants to check the fertile soil in which fanaticism grows has only to listen to the leader's responses to the assassination of [Dr. David] Gunn, the 47-year-old doctor and father of two. For example, Randall Terry . . . said, "We have to recognize that this doctor was a mass murderer."

Anthony Lewis of the *New York Times* quoted Terry at a rally in Melbourne, Florida, as saying, "We've found the weak link is the doctor. . . . We're going to expose them. We're going to humiliate them."

According to *Time*, "Doctors, their staffs and families find themselves stalked, harassed and threatened over the phone. . . . Even the children of clinic workers are targets." Thirteen-year-old Justin Merritt, whose mother is a counselor at a clinic in Melbourne, was approached by a girl and a woman in her thirties, picked up in a car, and driven to a restaurant. There they produced a Bible and told Justin that he and his mother were going to burn in hell. "They identified themselves as members of the anti-abortion group Operation Rescue," *Time* said, "and asked the boy whether he had names of patients at his mother's clinic."

When I testified before a Kansas Senate committee in March 1992 on behalf of religious liberty for women, including Roman Catholic women who sought abortions even though threatened with excommunication and ostracism, a young Catholic woman testified immediately following my statement. Between sobs she said that she had already given birth to two children and never dreamed she would seek an abortion. When the fetus she was carrying in her third trimester was diagnosed as having only about one-fourth of a heart and would die a painful death, she got no support from her priest and could not get a late-term abortion in Virginia.

When she arrived in Wichita, Kansas, to get the abortion, fanatical Operation Rescue demonstrators surrounded the bus in which she and others approached the clinic. Demonstrators shouting "Murderer" and "Baby Killer" imprisoned her on that bus for forty-eight hours. As she cried, she pleaded with the committee not to permit such actions again. When the public hearing ended, she threw her arms around me and thanked me for speaking for Roman Catholic women as well as for all women. She had spoken anonymously because, as a Catholic, she dared not give her name.

Some Roman Catholic bishops have participated in Operation Rescue actions designed to harass women and shut down clinics. An August 9, 1991, Associated Press story about the massive protest at the Wichita Family Planning Clinic said that eighty-one clergy members, most of them from Roman Catholic or evangelical churches, were arrested on trespassing charges. Bishop Eugene Gerber of the Roman Catholic diocese was not one of the 2,700 arrests made during the six-week blockade of clinics in Wichita.

Roman Catholic bishops cannot duck responsibility for Operation Rescue and similar groups. The bishops started the "right to life" movement. They started the idea that birth control just after conception is abortion and that abortion kills babies. They sought participation of other religious groups.

Jerry Falwell was one who responded, contributing $10,000 to Operation Rescue. New York Catholic Bishop Austin Vaughn joined the organization in 1988. And Pat Robertson, addressing the Wichita demonstrators, praised Operation Rescue's tactics there: "America owes these people not prison but a profound sense of gratitude."

Randall Terry is not only the apostle of violence but also the advocate of intolerance and hate. He is quoted in Jim Wallis's book *Who Speaks for God?* as saying:

> I want you just to let a wave of intolerance wash over you. I want you to let a wave of hatred wash over you. Yes, hate is good. . . .
> We have a biblical duty, we are called by God to conquer this country. We don't want equal time. We don't want pluralism.

No one can take lightly the candidacy of Randall Terry for Congress. Roman Catholic and evangelical church leaders who claim to be pro-life can be expected to support him, as they have done despite his practices and his statements about assassination. Already the *Wanderer* has printed his picture and the following caption as an endorsement:

> Randall Terry saved thousands of babies from abortion when he launched Operation Rescue in 1988. He galvanized and led tens of thousands of Christians to the abortion mills. Now he has the opportunity to bring his extraordinary leadership skills to bear on Congress. He's fighting to unseat a stubborn, hard-core, pro-abortion leader, a fight he can and must win.

With endorsements such as this, does anyone doubt that "pro-life" refers only to fetal life and not to the lives of women and doctors threatened by Randall Terry?

[Terry was roundly defeated in the Republican primary in 1998.]

THE 'PARTIAL-BIRTH' DEBATE IN 1998

As the 1998 elections draw near, the Republican-controlled Congress is expected to attempt another override of President Clinton's veto of the so-called Partial-Birth Abortion Act of 1997. After consulting with their religious allies, congressional Republican leaders will no doubt organize such an override attempt to take place on a date determined to have maximum impact on the elections.

Legislation prohibiting this particular type of late-term abortion first passed in the 1996 session of Congress and was vetoed by the president on the grounds that the bill permitted such abortions only if the mother's life were threatened, not if her health were in danger. It then became an issue in the presidential campaign of 1996, leading to new legislation by Congress and another presidential veto in 1997.

Given this continuing threat to reproductive freedom, it is compelling to review a few public cases of women whose lives would have been endangered had this legislation been law at the time of their pregnancies.

Vikki Stella from Naperville, Illinois. Parents of two daughters, Vikki and her husband Archer discovered at thirty-two weeks of pregnancy that the fetus had only fluid filling the cranium where its brain should have been, as well as other major problems. The Stellas made "the most loving decision we could have made" to terminate the pregnancy. Because the procedure preserved her fertility, Vikki was able to conceive again. In December 1995 she gave birth to a healthy boy, Nicholas.

Mary-Dorothy Line from Los Angeles, California. In the summer of 1995, Mary-Dorothy was told at twenty-one weeks of pregnancy that her fetus had an advanced, textbook case of hydrocephalus--an excess of fluid on the brain. It was so acute and so advanced that it was untreatable. Practicing Catholics, she and her husband Bill sought a medical miracle but were told that no surgery or therapy could save their baby. Indeed, the medical experts who received the case told her that her own health was at risk, and so the Lines decided to end the pregnancy. Mary-Dorothy was able to become pregnant again and gave birth to a healthy baby girl in September 1996.

Coreen Costello from Agoura, California. In April 1995, seven months pregnant with her third child, Coreen and her husband Jim found out that a lethal neuromuscular disease had left their much-wanted daughter unable to survive. Its body had stiffened and was frozen, wedged in a transverse

Reprinted by permission from The Humanist, *March/April 1998.*

position. In addition, amniotic fluid had puddled and built up to dangerous levels in Coreen's uterus. Devout Christians and opposed to abortion, the Costellos agonized for over two weeks about their decision and baptized the fetus in utero. Finally, Coreen's increasing health problems forced them to accept the advice of numerous medical experts that the intact dilation and extraction (D&X) was, indeed, the best option for Coreen's own health, and the abortion was performed. Later, in June 1996, Coreen gave birth to a healthy son.

Maureen Mary Britell from Sandwich, Massachusetts. Maureen and her husband Andrew, practicing Catholics, were expecting their second child in early 1994 when, at six months' gestation, a sonogram revealed that the fetus had anencephaly. No brain was developing, only a brain stem. Experts at the New England Medical Center in Boston confirmed that the fetus the Britells had named Dahlia would not survive. The Britells' parish priest supported their decision to induce labor and terminate the pregnancy. During the delivery, a complication arose and the placenta would not drop. The umbilical cord had to be cut, aborting the fetus while still in delivery in order to prevent serious health risks for Maureen. Dahlia had a Catholic funeral.

Claudia Crown Ades from Los Angeles, California. In 1992, in the twenty-sixth week of a desperately wanted pregnancy, Claudia and her husband Richard were told after an ultrasound that the male fetus she carried had a genetic condition called trisomy-13. Its anomalies included extensive brain damage, serious heart complications, and liver, kidney, and intestinal malformations. Its condition was incompatible with life. After consulting with many physicians, Claudia and Richard chose the D&X as the medically appropriate procedure for Claudia and the most compassionate procedure for their would-be son.

There are, of course, other cases wherein severely handicapped children would have been born had Congress succeeded in enacting the "partial-birth" legislation. The crucial question is whether medical decisions should be made by qualified physicians or by politicians.

The major medical associations oppose government intervention. The American College of Obstetricians and Gynecologists said, "The physician, in consultation with the patient, must choose the most appropriate method based upon the patient's individual circumstances." A legislative ban would force doctors in many cases to select what they consider a second-best method in order to avoid criminal prosecution.

Dr. Allan Rosenfield, an obstetrician and dean of New York's Columbia School of Public Health, says, "I am also concerned that the medical community is being used -- and abused -- to further the political agenda of individuals who do not support access to safe, legal abortion. To many this legislation appears to be simply the first step in a 'procedure by procedure' attempt to make the constitutional right to choose meaningless." The American Nurses Association concurred, stating, "It is inappropriate for the law to mandate a clinical course of action for a woman who is already faced with an intensely personal and difficult decision."

New Jersey lawyer John Tomasin has proposed that any such ban should include the following language:

PROVIDED:

(a) If the potential parents and best medical evidence clearly show that the potential child will probably be severely handicapped and unable to take care of itself for the rest of its life, and

(b)   The federal government forces the parents to have said child anyway, and

(c) If said child is in fact born severely handicapped and unable to take care of itself for the rest of its life,

(d) Then the federal government shall pay 51 percent of the costs of taking care of said child for the rest of its life, and, if the child is institutionalized, the federal government shall pay 100 percent of said costs, and

(e) If legal action is necessary to enforce such obligations, interested parties shall recover proper judgment, plus reasonable legal fees and costs.

Such a proposal, which would almost certainly be rejected, sheds light on the fact that the religious anti-abortion movement and its congressional allies are concerned only with religious doctrine and not with the consequences of the legislation they advocate and adopt.

The same motive is also responsible for perpetuating false information about the subject. For example, the term *partial-birth abortion*, which was used in the House and Senate bills, is not found in any medical dictionary or textbook. It is a term that originates in the anti-abortion movement, organized by the Catholic bishops and by the authors of the legislation in response to that movement. The Catholic bishops' "Plan for Pro-Life Activities" specifically demands "passage of federal and state laws and adoption of administrative policies that will restrict the practice of abortion as much as is possible."

It is also important to note that the anti-abortion movement always refers to embryos and fetuses as "babies." This is a propaganda device known as *prolepsis,* which *Webster's Dictionary* defines as "describing an event as if it has already happened" when, in fact, it may be months away or may never happen. For example, a normal person who eats a fertilized egg does not say,

"I have just eaten a chicken," nor is the crushing of an acorn the destruction of an oak tree.

In order to understand the meaning of *partial-birth abortion* it is essential to note that there are two types of abortion: elective and emergency. An elective abortion, which is chosen by the woman, must take place either in the first trimester (within twelve weeks of pregnancy) or in the second trimester (twenty-four weeks). The Supreme Court has held that a woman is constitutionally entitled to have an abortion of a nonviable fetus for whatever reasons she finds compelling. Therefore, physicians performing second-trimester abortions must first determine that the fetus is too underdeveloped to survive outside the womb.

After twenty-four weeks of pregnancy, which is the approximate date of viability and the beginning of the third trimester, the abortion procedure is not elective but emergency, in that the fetus is gravely or fatally impaired, or the woman's life or health is at risk, or both.

According to the most recent data, 90 percent of all abortions are performed in the first trimester and 99 percent within twenty weeks, or near the midpoint of the second trimester. No national data are available on abortions past twenty weeks, but the Allan Guttmacher Institute has estimated, based on limited data collected by the Centers for Disease Control and Prevention, that approximately 320 to 600 abortions annually are performed after the twenty-sixth week, hence, in the third trimester of pregnancy.

The term *partial-birth abortion* was defined in the 1996 legislation as one wherein "the person performing the abortion partially vaginally delivers a living fetus before killing the infant and completing the delivery." The nearest medical term that to some degree meets that definition is an *intact dilation and extraction*, which involves the deliberate dilation of the cervix, usually over a sequence of days. The fetal body, excepting the head, can then be readily extracted; the fetal head cannot until the doctor reduces the size so it can pass through the fragile and narrow cervical opening. That reduction requires partial evacuation of the intracranial contents.

This raises certain questions. Why is this procedure sometimes necessary? Why not induce labor with drugs? The cervix, which holds the uterus closed during pregnancy, is very resistant to dilation until about thirty-six weeks. Inductions done before this time take two to four days and are physically painful. Because of the danger of uterine rupture, the woman requires constant nursing supervision.

Another question: Isn't there another option, such as a caesarean section? A caesarean delivery usually involves twice as much blood loss and, before thirty-four weeks of pregnancy, the lower segment of the uterus is usually too thick to use a standard horizontal incision, so a vertical incision is necessary.

Any uterine incision complicates future pregnancy, but a vertical incision jeopardizes both the mother's health and future pregnancies, which would also require a caesarean.

The safest and, hence, better option in some situations is the D&X procedure. Using intravenous anesthesia, the physician can insert small dry cylinders into the cervix that expand gradually as they absorb fluid from the woman. She can usually return home except for twice-daily visits to the clinic or office to be sure that she is dilating and to replace the dilators if required. This, plus a spinal needle to remove some fluid from the fetal head, reduces the chance of lacerating the cervix.

There are still other questions, such as why not let the woman wait until the thirty-sixth week and go into labor? Fetuses with severe defects have a high chance of dying in utero well before labor begins and therefore create a serious threat to the mother. When a fetus dies, its tissues begin to break down and enter the mother's bloodstream. This can cause clotting problems, making it more difficult for her to stop bleeding. This may then require a surgical delivery or an emergency hysterectomy.

These and other problems are the reason the physician -- not the politician -- must be able to exercise judgment as to which method to pursue. The "partial-birth" legislation, however, makes the physician liable to criminal penalties if he or she chooses the D&X method, thus deterring doctors from using such procedures.

Dr. Rosenfield says, "The reasons these abortions are performed late [in the third trimester] is because these women were pursuing wanted pregnancies and then something went terribly wrong," such as "severe fetal abnormality" or serious health threats to the women that developed late in pregnancy.

All abortions require the termination of a fetus, but the government should not require a woman to bear an increased medical risk because one method of abortion may seem more brutal than another. Many medical decisions--ranging from invasive surgery to amputation--seem harsh but may be necessary to save a patient's life.

The focus of the original legislation, which President Clinton vetoed in 1996, was on catastrophic third-trimester pregnancies. It should be noted that the ban proposed in 1997 was not limited to the last few weeks of pregnancy, when one might expect a viable birth. Rather, it would ban D&X abortion in the second, as well as the third, trimester. Thus it is intended to ban abortions *before* viability as well as *after* viability.

It should be obvious that the abortion of a fetus well before viability cannot be a partial birth, because the fetus could not survive after the procedure. It is also true that some women during the second trimester need an abortion for medical, and not just elective, reasons. They therefore may need the same emergency care as if they were in the third trimester. However, the anti-abortion movement opposes all abortions--no matter what happens to the woman.

There is at least one other important argument against this legislation: one or a few religious organizations ought not to be able to legislate their religious dogma about abortion into law. If they are unable to persuade their own members not to have an abortion, they ought not use the police power of the state to send physicians to jail to prevent these women from having one. Nor should religious zealots be allowed to coerce women of other religions or no religion to accept *their* church's dogma. Separation of church and state is always better than theocracy.

POLITICS CENTERED UPON ABORTION

Many Americans were troubled by the injection of religion into the 1984 political campaign even if they didn't know why they were troubled. The Roman Catholic bishops, Jerry Falwell, and his fundamentalist Protestant colleagues had not broken the law. They were exercising their constitutional right of free speech. Religious commentary on political issues is also a long American tradition antedated by an even longer biblical history.

It is impossible in our society to be politically neutral without silently supporting the status quo. Political neutrality in a democracy means consent to numerous social injustices such as racial segregation, sexual discrimination, the use of the CIA to overthrow sovereign governments, and preparation for nuclear war.

The real issue is not whether religion is relevant to politics but what role, if any, the official leadership of a church should play in partisan politics. Bishop James W. Malone, President of the National Conference of Catholic Bishops, issued a statement, August 9, 1984, which said: "We reject the idea that candidates satisfy the requirements of rational analysis in saying their personal views should not influence their political decisions; the implied dichotomy -- between personal morality and public policy -- is simply not logically tenable in any adequate view of both." The bishop by this statement was referring to public comments by Governor Mario Cuomo and Vice Presidential candidate Geraldine Ferraro that they personally accepted their church's doctrine about abortion but that they did not believe in imposing by law their personal faith on the general population.

During the campaign many bishops were deeply involved in partisan politics. Cardinal Krol, for example, introduced President Reagan at a Polish-American Catholic shrine in Doylestown, Pa., and warmly praised him for having made a "sustained effort to reduce and eliminate the ugly blemish of injustice and discrimination" against parochial schools and for having shown "benevolence in providing aid for projects of the Catholic church in Poland." Archbishop John O'Connor of New York on several occasions singled out Geraldine Ferraro for attack and Bishop James Timlin of Scranton held a press conference to denounce Ferraro after she had spoken in Scranton. Various other bishops were similarly active at the partisan political level.

The Second Vatican Council appears to validate a conflicting personal moral view of politics. In a section dealing with participation in public life,

---

Reprinted by permission from The Churchman/Human Quest, *April, 1985.*

the Council said of candidates and officeholders: Those involved in politics "must dedicate themselves to the welfare of all in a spirit of sincerity and fairness, of love and of the courage demanded by political life."

A problem with the bishops' statement is that private religious convictions often do not establish the political consensus on which good law depends. This would certainly be true if Jews and Seventh-day Adventists were to seek to make Saturday instead of Sunday a legal holiday. The Catholic Bishops' position on abortion, according to public opinion polls, is held only by a minority of Americans. If a minority because of coalition building were victorious in the enactment of its religious doctrine, that would divide the nation, create disrespect for the law and for the church that inflicted its theological position on the people.

Another problem in the Bishops' statement was highlighted by Archbishop O'Connor in Altoona, Pa., when he quoted the Pope's statement: "The Church considers all legislation in favor of abortion a very serious offense . . . " O'Connor then said: "So Geraldine Ferraro doesn't have a problem with me. If she has a problem it's with the Pope." A bishop who puts pressure on Catholic candidates to achieve what the Pope wants in the United States is insensitive to the religious concerns of many Humanist, Jewish and Protestant citizens. O'Connor assumed that Catholic politicians do not serve the general public but must serve the Papacy and its doctrinal position. Loyalism differs from loyalty. Loyalism is a total commitment to another person or to an ecclesiastical office in spite of one's oath to defend the Constitution or to represent the people.

Another difficulty with the idea that private religious conviction must be translated into public policy is the assumption that if candidates holding the same religious convictions were to become a majority in government, there would be no freedom of conscience. When a church opposes the legalization or decriminalization of abortion or the sale of contraceptive birth control devices or the legal recognition of divorce, it demands more than a democratic secular state should grant. The state must not make something illegal because God or the Vicar of Christ forbids it. To ask the state to enforce God's will is to confuse church and state. It also confuses ethical obedience to one's faith with obedience derived from fear of the police.

The idea that individual personal morality or faith must be translated into public policy strikes at the heart of political and religious pluralism. In the United States we have come to believe that government is not the exclusive property of one faith, that government must be the protector of persons of every faith and of none, that non-Catholics can trust Catholic officeholders and Jews can trust Christian officeholders (and vice versa) to defend their religious liberty by not enforcing the faith or morals of any sectarian group.

Archbishop O'Connor said that he did not see "how a Catholic in good conscience can vote for a candidate who explicitly supports abortion." If Catholic citizens may not vote for candidates whose political position is different from the Bishop's then both candidates and individual Catholics are expected politically to conform to the hierarchy's position. They would presumably not be free to join politically active organizations that differ from the hierarchy on critical issues such as abortion. Does this mean that Catholic women may not join the National Organization of Women or a political party that supports free choice, or an educational association that opposes tuition tax credits? If this is the case, what happens to the American idea of freedom of association?

If Catholic candidates differ from the hierarchy on political issues are they to be subject to public attack and exposure as not being privately committed to the Church's position on sexual issues? Both Governor Cuomo and Rep. Ferraro felt impelled by public attack to state publicly their personal commitment to the sexual ethics of the hierarchy. Is this the end of privacy except for those Catholic politicians who publicly support the hierarchy's position but may privately or personally disregard it? Is public conformity more important than private commitment? The fatal error of authoritarian religious government and politics is that it does not respect either political or religious heresy and hence the dignity of the human person.

It is a serious matter if Catholic politicians who disagree with the hierarchy at some crucial point such as abortion or separation of church and state cannot run for office without being publicly attacked by their own church leaders. The expectation of political conformity plus the example of public attack on those who don't conform could have a chilling effect on the decision to run for office by potentially good public servants.

Neither personal nor political ethics can be based on rules applicable to the Middle Ages. Ethics varies according to the political and social context or according to time and circumstances. The medieval doctrine of the Just War created in the days of swords, bows and arrows and muskets seems to many of us to have little validity in the age of nuclear and other weapons of mass destruction. A doctrine which condemned abortion under all circumstances because it interferes with procreation and which assumes the obedience of women to a male hierarchy is not applicable to a society where women make and insist on making decisions about their lives, their health and their careers.

The hierarchy does not acknowledge the politically different context in which politicians operate or the pressures on women and their families that lead some to reject papal rules. But abortion is a doctrinal issue on which difference is not encouraged.

In order to avoid the charge that the bishops' political stance is a single issue, Cardinal Bernardin has coined the phrase "seamless robe" as if to imply that the bishops pay the same attention to war and poverty as to abortion. The Pope and bishops treat abortion and other sexual ethical issues with a far greater priority than any other topic except possibly aid to parochial schools. The 18 New England bishops said "while nuclear holocaust is a future possibility the abortion holocaust is a present reality." The strongest or the most colorful threads in the seamless robe are the abortion ones. Other issues are not doctrinal ones as abortion is.

Is there any solution to this problem of religion in partisan politics? James Madison in a discussion before the Virginia Convention in 1788 answered the question: Is a bill of rights necessary for religious liberty.

He said: "If there were a majority of one sect, a bill of rights would be a poor protection for liberty. Happily for the [United] States they enjoy the utmost freedom of religion. This freedom arises from the multiplicity of sects, which pervade America and which is the best and only security for religious liberty in any society. For where there is such a variety of sects there cannot be a majority of any one sect to oppress and persecute the rest."

Madison did not envision a day when Catholic bishops and Protestant fundamentalist leaders would join forces politically and when mainstream Protestants who had been involved in ecumenical dialog and action on other issues would remain silent for fear of offending Catholics or their leaders on abortion.

Madison did not envision a day when TV and radio would be the method of communication by which Jerry Falwell and other electronic preachers communicate with their followers who are isolated from each other and cannot express their doubts or argue their differences on issues with each other. Their congregations are passively obedient.

The Roman Catholic Church remains the same as in Madison's day with doctrines and morals passed down from the top to various congregations.

However, the dialog which Catholics and non-Catholics have with each other in the work-place and the commitment of most Catholic laity to separation of church and state and respect for the religious convictions of others is significant. It is also significant that the leadership of the 1800 member National Coalition of American Nuns announced in 1982 their opposition to laws forbidding abortion. (See *The Churchman*, December, 1984, p. 16.) Taking essentially the same position as Governor Cuomo and Geraldine Ferraro they said:

"While we continue to oppose abortion in principle and practice, we are likewise convinced that the responsibility for decisions in this regard resides primarily with those who are directly and personally involved."

Secular women's organizations take a position contrary to that of the bishops on abortion. Although a number of churches and other religious groups have adopted positions favoring a decriminalization of abortion they are not as vocal as Jerry Falwell and the bishops.

The solution is not one of trying to silence or condemn the bishops or the Moral Majority but of speaking out as vigorously for a different political position.

RIGHT-TO-LIFER MURDERS DOCTOR

The distinguished *New York Times* columnist, Anthony Lewis, wrote last March 12: "The murder of a doctor in Pensacola, Florida, tells us the essential truth about most anti-abortion activists. They are religious fanatics who want to impose their versions of God's word on the rest of us. For them the end justifies any means, including violence."

Dr. David Gunn, who was shot in the back by Michael Griffin at a Pensacola clinic, was a believer in women's rights and could recite the constitutional Bill of Rights from memory. His killer, Griffin, said *U.S.A. Today*, is described as "deeply religious and a member of Brownsville Assembly of God," the denomination of Jimmy Swaggart and Jim Bakker. Griffin had been in the Whitfield Assembly of God church in Berrydale, Florida, the preceding Sunday of the murder with John Burt, who led the group of protesters at the Pensacola clinic. Burt is the leader of "Rescue America," whose headquarters is in Houston, Texas.

Anthony Lewis reported, "Its national director, Don Tresham, said, 'While Gunn's death is unfortunate, it's also true that quite a number of babies' lives will be saved'."

Ellen Goodman wrote in a March 15 column, "Anyone who wants to check the fertile soil in which fanaticism grows has only to listen to the leaders' responses to the assassination of the 47-year-old doctor and father of two. For example, Randall Terry of 'Operation Rescue' said, 'We have to recognize that this doctor was a mass murderer'."

Anthony Lewis quoted Terry as saying at a rally in Melbourne, Florida: "We've found the weak link is the doctor. . . . We're going to expose them. We're going to humiliate them." Don Treshham was reported in *Time* as saying of the murder of Dr. Gunn: "This will have a chilling effect on this business."

"Doctors, their staffs and families," said *Time*, "find themselves stalked, harassed and threatened over the phone. . . . Even the children of clinic workers are targets." A 13-year-old boy, Justin Merritt, whose mother, Lisa, is a counselor at a clinic in Melbourne, was approached by a girl and a woman in her thirties, picked up in a car, and driven to a restaurant. There they produced a Bible and told Justin that he and his mother were going to burn in hell. "They identified themselves as members of the anti-abortion group Operation Rescue and asked the boy whether he had names of patients

---

Reprinted by permission from The Churchman/Human Quest, *May-June 1993.*

at his mother's clinic."

The Rev. Joseph Foreman, co-founder of Missionaries to the Preborn, thinks of harassment of women and doctors and damage to clinics as moderate action and described Operation Rescue as a moderate organization. In a March 18 column by Molly Ivins he is quoted as saying, "It is a universal fact of history. Wherever the moderates have been crushed and swept from the street, the way is paved for the true extremists like Michael Griffin to step up to the plate. Abortion industry, you won in Pensacola; you ran the activists off. Now you deal with the next phase of the anti-abortion movement."

Some Roman Catholic bishops have participated in Operation Rescue actions designed to harass women and shut down clinics. An Associated Press story of August 9, 1991, about the massive protest at the Wichita Family Planning Clinic, said that 81 clergy members were arrested on trespassing charges, most of them from Catholic or evangelical churches. Bishop Eugene Gerber of the Catholic diocese was not arrested.

When I testified before a Kansas Senate Committee in March of 1992 on behalf of religious liberty for women, including Catholic women who sought abortions even though threatened with excommunication and ostracism, a beautiful young Catholic woman testified immediately following my statement. Between sobs she said she had already given birth to two children and never dreamed she would seek an abortion. When the fetus she was carrying in her third trimester was diagnosed as having only about one-fourth of a heart and would die a painful death, she got no support from her priest and could not get a late abortion in Virginia.

When she arrived in Wichita to get a late abortion, fanatical Operation Rescue demonstrators surrounded the bus in which she and others approached the clinic. Demonstrators shouting "Murderer" and "Baby killer" imprisoned her on that bus for 48 hours. As she cried she pleaded with the committee not to permit such actions again.

When the public hearing ended, she threw her arms around me and thanked me for speaking for Roman Catholic women as well as for all women. She spoke anonymously, as she dared not as a Catholic give her name.

One of the few Catholic groups that openly condemned the killing of Dr. Gunn in Pensacola is the Sisters of Loretto Women's Network. They said, "Responsibility for this death must be borne by all groups whose language around this issue calls forth violence and highly emotional responses." They called upon all "religious groups, including our own church" to "condemn vandalism, bombings, arson attempts, assaults, and invasions in and around the clinics, and urge legislation protecting the rights of women to receive appropriate medical procedures without outside interference."

The U.S. Catholic Conference said, "The violence of killing in the name of pro-life makes a mockery of the pro-life cause." Unfortunately, no cardinal or bishop, so far as I have been able to discover, has ever publicly condemned the long series of violent acts that led to the killing.

The *Kansas City Star* reported "186 clear cases of vandalism, bombings, arson attempts, or assaults and invasions in 1992 compared to 93 in 1991." The *Star* editorial of March 12 said, "You cannot go around shouting 'murderer' at people who are acting within the law and providing a legal service without provoking a frenzied response."

The Catholic bishops cannot duck responsibility for Operation Rescue and similar groups. They started the "right to life" movement and the idea that birth control just after conception is abortion and abortion kills babies. They sought participation of other religious groups. Jerry Falwell was one who responded. He said in an interview in the *San Francisco Focus*, February 1988, "I went to see some Catholic leaders and political people in Washington and then formed the Moral Majority."

Operation Rescue is the brainchild of Joseph Scheidler who is said to have prepared for the Roman Catholic priesthood. His fundamentalist Protestant disciple, Randall Terry, is the national leader of Operation Rescue. Jerry Falwell contributed $10,000 to Operation Rescue, and a New York Catholic bishop, Austin Vaughn, joined the organization in 1988. Pat Robertson addressed the Wichita rally during Operation Rescue's action there and said of the terrorist attacks: "America owes these people not prison but a profound sense of gratitude." About 2700 arrests had been made during that six-week blockade of clinics.

Much of the religious leadership of America either provokes the violence against women, doctors and clinics or gives assent to it by silence. Cardinal O'Connor, perhaps the chief leader of the anti-abortion movement, has made abortion the most important Catholic issue. His newspaper, *Catholic New York*, on April 9, 1992, stated: "Cardinal O'Connor asserted that unless rebutted, attacks on the church's stand on abortion effectively erode its authority on 'all matters . . . indeed on the authority of God Himself."

Anthony Lewis commented: "In this country we have a constitutional bargain about religion. Individuals are guaranteed the right to choose their faith, but they may not compel others to accept their views -- that the Bible as they interpret it is law, for example, or that barely formed fetuses are human beings. The bargain is essential to our form of democracy, which requires compromise and does not work when there are ideological certainties."

It is religious and ideological dogmatism that fuels the right-to-life movement.

ABORTION SURVEY: THE ECONOMIC FACTOR

The controversy about abortion has generally ignored one of the major factors causing abortion: poverty or economic insecurity. It is assumed by many Americans that any reason for abortion other than rape, incest or preservation of the life of the woman is "abortion for convenience." Middle class people who do not live on the poverty level often do not distinguish economic necessity from convenience. It is not convenience but necessity when a woman has no way to support a child.

A majority in a survey of more than 10,000 women who had abortions in 1987, according to a report in the October 6, 1988, *New York Times,* said they could not afford to have a baby or that a baby would interfere with their work or schooling to prepare for work.

Women whose family income was less than $11,000 were almost four times as likely to have abortions as women with family incomes of more than $25,000, according to a report in the April 6, 1989, *Kansas City Star.*

A woman who scarcely knows where the next meal for herself or her children is coming from does not have the same freedom to choose childbirth as does a woman whose income is $20,000 or more a year. Although each woman's situation is different, the following statistics will give a picture of the problems confronting poor women and their families. Many families in our society are without fathers. As of spring, 1986, 8.8-million mothers were living with children whose fathers were absent from the home. Sixty-one percent, or 5.4-million, of those women had been awarded child support payments, but one-fourth of those received only partial payment and another fourth received nothing. Nearly one-third of the women heading single-parent families, or 2.8-million women, had incomes below the poverty level in 1985.

Fourteen million women of childbearing age have no health insurance. In 1985, more than 11-million children under 18 were completely uninsured. The Physicians Task Force on Hunger in America estimated in 1985 that 20-million Americans go hungry at some point each month, and that malnutrition affects almost 500,000 American children.

The choice for abortion of a woman who works at a minimum wage and is already supporting one or more children, or possibly an unemployed husband or parent, is already largely conditioned by the economic instability of her family. From 1979 to 1985, the number of Americans paid on an hourly basis at wages so low that full-time work could not lift a family of

Reprinted by permission from The Churchman/Human Quest, *May-June 1990.*

three out of poverty, jumped from 2.8-million to more than 10.6-million. Full-time year-round work at the minimum wage (which has been $3.35 per hour for years) now yields annual earnings that are less than three-fourths of what is needed to lift a family of three out of the poverty level of $9,300.

Many women, especially teenagers, cannot afford prenatal medical care or the cost of a child. Even an abortion is costly. Since 1977 virtually no federal Medicaid funds have been available for abortions for poor women, although in 1985, fourteen states and the District of Columbia covered the costs of 187,500 abortions for poor women. The average charge for non-hospital abortions at ten weeks in 1986 was $238.

Some women who lack Medicaid funding borrow the money, cut down on groceries, or work at extra jobs or overtime to get an abortion. This often delays the procedure until they get the money. If this puts them into the second trimester, both financial costs and medical risks are likely to be greater. Many women, of course, cannot borrow or are unemployed.

Members of families with children now represent more than one-third of the homeless population nationwide. In New York City in September, 1987, 12,000 homeless children were more than the total number of homeless single men and women combined. In Trenton, New Jersey, and Providence, Rhode Island, at least 50% of the homeless people in 1987 were members of families with children.

In fifteen states in 1985 the entire monthly aid to families with dependent children (AFDC) for a family of four was less than the federally-estimated low fair market rent for the area. For example, the median rent in Louisiana was $321 a month, but the maximum AFDC benefit for a family of three in that state was $190.

There are many single-parent families headed by women who have never married. Of these women with children living below the poverty level, 50% have never been married, compared with 22% of all women with children.

Marriage rates for all Americans aged 20 to 21 fell by 46% between 1974 and 1985. More than a fourth of the drop in marriage rates among high school graduates and nearly half of the decline among dropouts can be tied directly to declining earnings among young men. It did not, however, prevent sexual relationships.

In 1985, an estimated one-million teenagers became pregnant in the U.S. Fewer than half (477,705) resulted in births; an estimated 13% ended in miscarriage, and an estimated 40% in abortions. Of the teenage mothers who give birth to 1,300 babies each year, 800 have not completed high school, and 199 have not completed ninth grade. Each day, twenty-six 13- and 14-year-olds and 460 teenage girls between 15 and 17 years have their first child, and thirteen 16-year-olds have their second child.

There is a correlation between teenage pregnancy, school dropouts, and poverty. Forty percent of teenage girls who drop out of school do so because of pregnancy or marriage. Only half of the teens who become parents before age 18 graduate.

Such statistics about poverty, teenage pregnancy, school dropouts, low wages, and other economic problems in our society suggest that there is a systemic connection between poverty and abortion.

The late Episcopal Bishop of St. Louis, Missouri, George Leslie Cadigan, wisely said: "The 'rightness' or 'wrongness' of abortion as the solution of a problem pregnancy is not the critical issue here. The issue is the larger ethical one: can any one of us stand in the role of judge for the personal decisions of others? What robes shall we wear? Greater than the debatable immorality of terminating an undesired pregnancy is the immorality of refusing a woman access to medical help when she has determined that she needs it."

Abortions can be minimized by dealing with economic and educational problems in our society. They cannot be eliminated by laws prohibiting abortions or by punishing women who have them and physicians who perform them.

TOO MANY PEOPLE, TOO FEW RESOURCES

The United Nations Fund for Population Activities (UNFP) in 1991 stated: "World population, which reached 5.4 billion in mid-1991, is growing faster than 250,000 every day. At the beginning of the decade the annual addition was 93 million; by the end of the nineties it will approach 100 million. At this rate the world will have almost a billion more people (roughly the population of China) by the year 2001."

So urgent is the slowing of population growth that a joint statement was issued recently by the officers of the Royal Society of London and the National Academy of Sciences of the United States which in summary says: "If current predictions of population growth prove accurate and patterns of human activity on the planet remain unchanged, science and technology may not be able to prevent either irreversible degradation of the environment or continued poverty for much of the world."

However, an organization more powerful than any of the above organizations has used its influence with major governments to prevent discussion of overpopulation and funding of family planning programs. *The New York Times* reported on May 28, "In preparation for next month's Earth Summit in Rio de Janeiro, Vatican diplomats have begun a campaign to try to insure that the gathering's conclusions on the issue of runaway population growth are not in conflict with Roman Catholic teaching on birth control."

"Family Planning" References Opposed

According to the same report, "officials said Vatican diplomats insisted on changing the wording in references to 'family planning' to the formulation: 'the responsible planning of family size in keeping with fundamental dignity and personally held values and taking into account ethical and cultural considerations'."

This "more cumbersome wording," said *The New York Times,* "reflects the Roman Catholic Church's prohibition on all forms of artificial birth control."

The World Council of Churches (WCC), representing Protestant and Orthodox churches, spoke most strongly at Rio on the population control issue. In a meeting held June 1 in one of Rio's most poverty stricken areas with 176 church representatives from around the world, WCC General

Reprinted by permission from Christian Social Action, *November 1992.*

Secretary Emilio Castro said, "While the Catholic Church is against the methodology of using artificial birth control to decrease population growth, the WCC believes that the responsibility of choosing the methodology belongs to the couple."

Following that meeting, the WCC issued a document which said: " . . . family planning information and services ought to be available as a basic right. Women, in particular, have a right to reproductive freedom and the conditions in which choice is possible."

However, on June 13 the Vatican secretary of state, Cardinal Angelo Sodano, addressed the Earth Summit's plenary body, stating the Vatican's official position: "Everyone is aware of the problems that can come from a disproportionate growth of the world's population. The Church is aware of the complexity of the problem, but the urgency of the situation must not lead into error in proposing ways of intervening. To apply methods which are not in accord with the true nature of man actually ends up by causing tragic harm . . . "

An effective response to the Vatican insistence that the world accept its method of "natural family planning" was made by an editorial in the June 19 *National Catholic Reporter:* "What constitutes 'artificial'? Are thermometers, wall charts and litmus papers less artificial than other birth regulation devices? Is it always more 'moral' to control birth by natural-family-planning methods, even for selfish reasons (to put aside the nest egg for a home on the ocean) than to limit it by, say, condoms, for selfish reasons (avoiding another infant death from starvation)?"

"Great Harm to the Planet"

The editor, Tom Fox, also said: "I feel the church is causing great harm to the planet, making millions suffer unnecessarily, and is compromising its teaching authority to boot, by its absolutist, narrowly defined birth-control position."

The harm caused by the Vatican can be measured. The same editorial said, "Among today's 5.2 billion, as many as one-fifth, mostly children, are undernourished. About 15 million die from hunger or hunger-related causes yearly."

The editorial reported, "It was the work of mostly Latin American countries, marshaled by the Vatican, which succeeded in removing birth control from the June 3-14 Conference's agenda."

The controversy over birth control and family planning as related to overpopulation will not go away. In an unprecedented attack on the White House, the highly respected Sierra Club said in July that the President has vetoed "two foreign aid budgets in order to block all US funding for the United Nations Fund for Population Activities" and thus "the US becomes the only major country not to fund the UN's population program."

The Sierra Club not only links President Bush's policy to "the urging of the Vatican" but asserts that "during President Bush's four years in office, 52 million children under the age of five died, many from preventable causes linked to pollution. Some 300 million couples are without access to family planning services."

All Natural Resources Diminishing

In order to defend doctrines against family planning, contraception and also abortion, the Vatican and some others say there is enough arable land and food potential to feed ever larger populations. The problem is not land, but all natural resources. Fresh water is limited.

"People withdraw the equivalent of Lake Huron from the world's rivers, streams, lake and aquifers each year, and withdrawals have been increasing 4 to 8 percent a year in recent decades. . . . " wrote William K. Stevens in the May 5 *New York Times*. "Supplies of water are beginning to fall behind demand in northern China and the World Resources Institute says shortages could reach crisis proportions in the Middle East before this decade is out. Shortages have become a familiar and serious problem in the southwestern United States, particularly in California."

The shortage of water in the Mideast is illustrative. "'No matter what progress irrigated agriculture makes, Jordan's natural water at this pace will be exhausted in 2010,' predicted Elias Salameh, founder and former director of the University of Jordan's Water Research and Study Center," according to the May 14 *Washington Post*. "'Jordan then will be totally dependent on rain water and will revert to desert. Its ruin will destabilize the entire region.'"

Salameh continued, "'None of the regional countries -- Egypt, Israel, Jordan, Syria, Saudi Arabia or the Gulf Emirates can be self-sufficient in food in the foreseeable future, if ever. All Middle East economies must be restructured away from agriculture because of a lack of water."

In southern Africa "eleven countries with a population of more than 120 million are living under a drought previously unknown to the region in its sweep and severity. . . . Lakes have dried up. . . . 17 million people are now under direct threat of starvation," wrote Anthony Lewis in the July 10 *New York Times*.

Tropical Forest Disappearing

Humans also use other indispensable resources: "The population explosion in the developing countries has intensified the pressure on forests . . . which are one of the last sources of fuel and of new pasture and arable land, however marginal," wrote William Stevens. "As a result, according to United Nations estimates, an area of tropical forest larger than the state of Florida is disappearing each year. . . . Worldwide, scientists say there has been a net loss of more than 3 million square miles of forest, an area roughly equal to the 8 contiguous states of the United States. About half the loss has come since 1850."

Stevens added: "Trees play a vital role in the maintenance of the biosphere. They hold soil in place, preventing erosion and the silting of rivers. They absorb water and give off moisture, helping to recycle water. They absorb vast amounts of heat-trapping carbon dioxide and lock it up in their cells."

"We have got to realize that next to the human mind, the earth's biological wealth is the greatest thing about this planet," said James Gustave Speth, president of World Resources Institute, a Washington organization. As many as 50 plant species disappear each day, steadily reducing the planet's biodiversity. The implications for human health are enormous. As James Brooks noted in the February 11 *New York Times:* "One fourth of all prescriptions now dispensed in the United States contain active ingredients from plants. . . . Threats to the world's gene pool come from headlong expansion of human society."

Family Planning Services Opposed

There is little question that Vatican dogma against family planning and the Reagan-Bush administrations' acceptance of this for political purposes are major factors in the population crisis. The Pope travels throughout Africa, Latin America, and other parts of the world condemning birth control and family planning. The Reagan-Bush administrations, as *Time* magazine reported February 24, gave worldwide political implementation to the Vatican's religious position. The *London Economist* noted, "At present roughly 300 million couples worldwide say they want family planning services but cannot get them. In Bolivia and Ghana, for example, 35 percent of couples complain that they do not have the contraceptives they want."

The Sierra Club, one of the most respected US environmental organizations, in a July 9 release, said, "While the Bush administration is spending time attacking fictional television characters for political gain, real people are dying of famine, disease, and environmental degradation. Leadership through adequate funding of population assistance could have prevented many of these tragedies."

Obviously the Pope and the President are not solely responsible for unintended pregnancies, unwanted children, and the world population explosion. Too many who know better have acquiesced in their policies. Nor is the population problem a Catholic-Protestant battle. Millions of Roman Catholics in the United States and Western Europe, as well as Jews, Protestants and the Orthodox and unchurched, are advocates both of family planning and population control.

Ann Quindlen, a *New York Times* columnist, writing about the Earth Summit, noted on June 10, "The ban on birth control espoused by the Catholic Church -- but ignored by millions of its own people -- has shaped the summit for those of all faiths."

It has become increasingly evident that Americans should not permit the Vatican to go unchallenged in its opposition to birth and population control. We can do this best by giving our own vocal support of US funding of family planning as an important measure that can deal with unintended pregnancies, burgeoning population, and poverty.

Appendix I

IN THE
SUPREME COURT OF THE UNITED STATES
OCTOBER TERM, 1988

No. 88-605

WILLIAM L. WEBSTER, et al.,
Appellants,
v.

REPRODUCTIVE HEALTH SERVICES, et al.,
Appellees.

**On Appeal from the United States Court of Appeals
for the Eighth Circuit**

AMICI CURIAE **BRIEF OF
167 DISTINGUISHED SCIENTISTS AND PHYSICIANS,
INCLUDING 11 NOBEL LAUREATES,
IN SUPPORT OF APPELLEES**

DESCRIPTION AND INTEREST OF AMICI CURIAE

Amici are distinguished scientists and physicians having specialized training and expertise in, among others, the fields of developmental biology, neurobiology, molecular biology and obstetrics and gynecology. Amici have been recognized for their contributions to their respective fields. Eleven[*] of *amici*, for example, have been awarded the Nobel Prize in their respective disciplines. A complete list of *amici* and their professional affiliations appears in the Appendix.

Amici have observed that appellants and some *amici* urging that *Roe v. Wade*, 410 U.S. 113 (1973), be overruled have purported to ground their arguments, in part, upon alleged scientific "truth." For example, appellants characterize the proposition that life begins at conception as a "biological fact," comparable to the "truth" that the "Earth still moves around the sun." (Brief for Appellants, p. 26.) Other *amici* aligned with appellants have asserted that subsequent advancements in science since *Roe v. Wade* was decided have rendered the decision obsolete.

Actually, 12 Nobel laureates signed this brief. One simply omitted the award from his c.v.

As scientists, *amici* have a special ability to provide the Court with accurate scientific information bearing upon such arguments. *Amici* also have a unique interest in seeing that scientific learning is not distorted or misused in arguments concerning abortion. Accordingly, amici submit this brief supporting appellees.

SUMMARY OF ARGUMENT

There is no scientific consensus that a human life begins at conception, at a given stage of fetal development, or at birth. The question of "when a human life begins" cannot be answered by reference to scientific principles like those with which we predict planetary movement. The answer to that question will depend on each individual's social, religious, philosophical, ethical and moral beliefs and values.

Science can, however, provide answers to certain concrete questions regarding prenatal development that have arisen in the controversy over abortion and *Roe v. Wade*, 410 U.S. 113 (1973). For example, appellants and several amici assert that medical advances are undermining *Roe v. Wade* by moving the point of fetal viability briskly and inexorably toward the date of conception. Science is capable of addressing--and in this case refuting--such arguments.

The earliest point of viability has remained virtually unchanged at approximately 24 weeks of gestation since 1973, and there is no reason to believe that a change is either imminent or inevitable. The reason that viability has not been pushed significantly back toward the point of conception is that critical organs, particularly lungs and kidneys, do not mature before that time. Progress in science, therefore, has not made obsolete the trimester framework based on viability articulated in *Roe v. Wade*. The trimester framework, moreover, corresponds with another aspect of fetal development--the chronology of human brain development. Not until after 28 weeks of gestation does the fetus attain sufficient neocortical complexity to exhibit those sentient capacities that are present in full-term newborns. In lay terms, the capacity for the human thought process as we know it cannot exist until sometime after 28 weeks of gestation.

This Court's decision in *Roe v. Wade* is as well grounded in "biological justifications," 410 U.S. at 163, today as in 1973, and the basic chronology of human development recognized in the Court's opinion remains accurate. Accordingly, the Court should reject arguments for overruling the decision because of alleged inconsistency with scientific advancement or "truth."

ARGUMENT

I. THERE IS NO SCIENTIFIC CONSENSUS ON WHEN A HUMAN LIFE BEGINS

Appellants and several *amici* aligned with them argue that the controversy over abortion and *Roe v. Wade*, 410 U.S. 113 (1973), may be resolved by what they contend is scientific "truth." Appellants, for example, contend that, as surely as "[t]he Earth still moves around the sun," it is an undisputed "biological fact" that a human life begins at conception.[1] Certain *amici* likewise argue that *Roe v. Wade* is contrary to an alleged "scientific truth" or "fact" that life begins at conception.[2] Others cite alleged technological advances as the justification for reconsidering and overruling *Roe v. Wade*.[3]

Amici submit that such arguments are an attempt to distort the teachings of science to fit preconceived conclusions based upon values that science alone does not and cannot dictate. The question of when a human life begins cannot be answered with reference to a scientific law or principle, such as the empirically-testable propositions with which we predict planetary movement. Individual scientists will have individual answers to that question, based upon their individual values and beliefs. These answers do not represent any "scientific" truth, because they are based upon values and beliefs, not upon science alone.

The only "consensus" that may be said to exist among scientists on the question of when a human life begins is that science alone cannot answer that question. This is demonstrated by the response of the scientific community when in 1981 a Senate subcommittee held hearings on a bill to declare "that present day scientific evidence indicates a significant likelihood that actual human life exists from conception." *See The Human Life Bill: Hearings Before the Subcommittee on Separation of Powers of the Senate Committee on the Judiciary,* 97th Cong., 1st Sess. (1981) [hereinafter *Hearings*]. As distinguished scientists testified, science alone does not provide the answer to this question.

For example, Dr. Leon Rosenberg, then Chairman of the Department of Human Genetics, Yale University Medical School, and a signatory of this brief, testified:

> When does this potential for human life become actual? As a scientist, I must answer I do not know. Moreover, I have not been able to find a single piece of scientific evidence which helps me with that question.
>
> Not surprisingly, a great deal has been spoken and written on the subject. Some people argue, as you have heard, that life begins at conception. . . .
>
> I have no quarrel with anyone's ideas on this matter so long as it is clearly understood that they are personal beliefs based on personal judgments and not scientific truths.

---

[1] Brief for Appellants at 26.

[2] *See, e.g.,* Brief *Amicus Curiae* of Hon. Christopher H. Smith, Hon. Alan B. Mollohan, Hon. John C. Danforth, and Other United States Senators and Members of Congress at 21; Brief *Amici Curiae* of Doctors for Life, Missouri Nurses for Life, and Lawyers for Life, Inc. at 21-23; *Amicus* Alabama Lawyers for Unborn Children, Inc. at 13-17; Brief for *Amicus Curiae*, The New England Christian Action Council, Inc. at 7.

[3] *See, e.g.,* Brief for the United States as *Amicus Curiae* at 19; Brief of the Knights of Columbus as *Amicus Curiae* at 6.

Id. at 50.

Dr. Rosenberg then explained the reason science alone cannot answer the question--the inability to test the hypothesis by the scientific method:

> The scientific method depends on two essential things--a thesis or idea and a means of testing that idea. Scientists have been able to determine, for instance, that the Earth is round or that genes are composed of DNA because, and only because, experiments could be performed to test these ideas. Without experiments there is no science, no way to prove or disprove any idea. I maintain that concepts such as humanness are beyond the purview of science because no idea about them can be tested experimentally.

Id.

The National Academy of Sciences was equally emphatic:

> It is the view of the National Academy of Sciences that the statement in [Senate Bill S. 158] cannot stand up to the scrutiny of science. This section reads, "The Congress finds that present day scientific evidence indicates a significant likelihood that actual human life exists from conception." This statement purports to derive its conclusions from science, but it deals with a question to which science can provide no answer. The proposal in S158 that the term "person" shall include "all human life" has no basis within our scientific understanding. Defining the time at which the developing embryo becomes a person must remain a matter of moral or religious value.

Id. at 74. *See also id.* at 1035-36 (statement of Joseph Boyle, M.D., chairman of the board of trustees of the American Medical Association) (there is no scientific consensus that a human life begins at conception; that question goes "far beyond the realm of medical science and into social, religious, philosophical, ethical, and moral concerns").

As shown in the next section of this brief, science can indeed provide valuable information and can answer concrete questions regarding prenatal development by identifying, for example, the stages of fetal brain development. But the question of when a human life truly begins calls for a conclusion as to which characteristics define the essence of human life. While science can tell us when certain biological attributes can be detected, science cannot tell us which biological attributes establish the existence of a human being.

Many other physicians and scientists made these observations at the 1981 hearings. *See, e.g., id.* at 68 (statement of Robert H. Ebert, M.D., President of Milbank Memorial Fund, Caroline Shields Walker Professor of Medicine Emeritus, Harvard University) (whether a human life begins at conception is not a medical or scientific question, but a philosophical and religious question that "can be debated endlessly and has to do with how one defines a person and 'self'"); *id.* at 69-70 (statement of Sherman M. Mellinkoff, M.D., Dean of the UCLA School of Medicine) (same); *id.* at 71 (statement of Arno G. Motulsky, M.D., Professor of Medicine and Genetics, University of Washington) (same); *id.* at 113-14 (statement of Dr. Jessica G. Davis, Director, Child Development Center, Chief, Division of Genetics, North Shore University Hospital) (same). The subcommittee also received hundreds of letters from scientists and physicians across the country echoing Dr. Rosenberg's views. *See e.g., Hearings app.* at 414, 669, 716, 718.[4]

Science cannot define the essential attributes of human life any more than science can define such concepts as love, faith or trust. *Hearings* at 50. This Court was indisputably correct when it observed in *Roe v. Wade*, 410 U.S. at 159, that the question of when a human life begins cannot simply be referred to an expert discipline for resolution.

Science can, however, offer to this controversy concrete information concerning the physiology of prenatal development--particularly, scientific observations about viability and brain development. As shown below, these observations support the chronology of fetal development recognized in *Roe v. Wade*.

II. ROE V. WADE HAS NOT BEEN RENDERED OBSOLETE BY SUBSEQUENT ADVANCEMENTS IN SCIENCE

Appellants and several *amici*, including the United States, cite developments in science and technology as a justification for reconsidering and overruling 410 U.S. 113 (1973). Citing Justice O'Connor's dissenting opinion in *Roe v. Wade,* 410 U.S. 113 (1973). Citing Justice O'Connor's dissenting opinion *in City of Akron v. Akron Center for Reproductive Health,* 462 U.S. 416, 456-58 (1983), these litigants and aligned amici suggest that there has been enormous movement in the point of viability since 1973.[5] Although Justice O'Connor's opinion in *Akron* stated that "fetal viability

---

[4] The fact that the subcommittee itself could not reach agreement on the question further highlights the inability to find the answer in scientific truth. *The Human Life Bill--S. 158: Report by the Subcommittee on Separation of Powers, Senate Committee on the Judiciary*, 97th Cong., 1st Sess. 39, 41 (1981) (minority view of Senator Baucus) ("If the hearings on S. 158 held by the Separation of Powers Subcommittee were conclusive on any point it is that in 1981 there remains no consensus among scientists, philosophers and theologians on the question of when life begins"). Indeed, the current Commissioner of the Food and Drug Administration, Frank E. Young, M.D., stated in 1981 that "science and medicine cannot unequivocally establish the time in the continuum of development where human life begins"; the decision is "in part moral, ethical, philosophical and religious." *Hearings app.* at 781.

[5] *See, e.g.,* Brief for Appellants at 12-14; Brief for the United States as *Amicus Curiae* at 19; Brief of the Association for Public Justice, and the Value of Life Committee, Inc., as *Amici Curiae* at 25; Brief of Catholics United for Life, National Organization of Episcopalians for Life, Presbyterians Pro-Life, American Baptist Friends of Life, Baptists for Life, Southern Baptists for Life, Lutherans for Life, Moravians for Life, United Church of Christ Friends for Life, Task Force of United Methodists on Abortion and Sexuality, and the Christian Action Council as *Amici Curiae* at 19, 21.

in the first trimester of pregnancy may be possible in the not too distant future," *id.* at 457 (emphasis added), these advocates have tried to use her observations to catapult themselves to the conclusion that the point of viability is marching briskly and inexorably toward the date of conception because of technological change.[6]

Assertions that viability has moved significantly earlier in fetal development are flatly contrary to the scientific evidence. Although advances in technology have improved the chances of survival for premature birth *within* the range of 24 to 28 weeks, the *outer limit* of viability at 24 weeks has not significantly changed. Moreover, there is no reason to believe that a change in this outer limit is either imminent or inevitable.

A. The Point of Viability Has Not Changed Significantly Since 1973 And Such Change Is Not Likely To Occur In The Foreseeable Future

In *Roe v. Wade,* 410 U.S. at 160, this Court recognized that viability occurs at approximately 24 to 28 weeks of gestation. In *Colautti v. Franklin*, 439 U.S. 379 (1979), the Court emphasized that the date of viability was not intended to be fixed and arbitrary, but rather left "flexible for anticipated advancements in medical skill." Id. at 397. The Court further stated: "Viability is reached when, in the judgment of the attending physician on the particular facts of the case before him, there is a reasonable likelihood of the fetus' sustained survival outside the womb, with or without artificial support." *Id.* at 388.

Since *Roe v. Wade* was decided, great strides have been made in medicine, but the significance of those strides should not be misunderstood. Advances in medical technology have enhanced the probability of survival of infants born prematurely at 24 weeks and later. *See, e.g.,* Gerdes, Abbasi, Bhutani & Bowen, *Improved Survival and Short-Term Outcome of Inborn "Micropremies,"* 25 Clinical Pediatrics 391, 393 (1986); Buckwald, Zorn & Egan, *Mortality and Follow-up Data for Neonates Weighing 500 to 800 g at Birth,* 138 American Journal of Diseases of Children 779 (1984); Pleasure, Dhand & Kaur, *What is the Lower Limit of Viability,* 138 American Journal of Diseases of Children 783 (1984).

However, these advances have not significantly changed the earliest date of viability, which remains approximately at the 24-week mark recognized in *Roe v. Wade*. See, e.g., Pleasure, Dhand & Kaur, *What is the Lower Limit of Viability*, 138 American Journal of Diseases of Children 783 (1984); Milner & Beard, Limit of Fetal Viability, 1 Lancet 1079 (1984); Koops, Morgan & Bataglia, *Neonatal Mortality Risk in Relation to Birth Weight and Gestational Age: Update,* 101 Journal of Pediatrics 969-77 (1982). Thus, the scientific evidence supports the finding made by the District Court:

Testimony by medical experts for both plaintiffs and defendants, in addition to recent medical literature, provides clear evidence that 23 1/2 to 24 weeks

---

[6] See, e.g, Brief for Appellants at 12-14.

gestation is the earliest point in pregnancy where a reasonable probability of viability exists.

Reproductive Health Services v. Webster, 662 F. Supp. 407, 420 (W.D. Mo. 1987) (citations omitted).

The reason that viability has not advanced to a point significantly earlier than 24 weeks of gestation is that critical organs, particularly the lungs and kidneys, do not mature before that time. While a number of factors, such as immaturity of the immune system, contribute to the mortality rate for premature infants, the most important determinant of viability is lung development--specifically, the development of the air sacs through which gases are passed into and out of the blood stream.

Air sac development sufficient for gas exchange does not occur until at least 23 weeks after gestation and often later. Report of the Committee on Fetal Extrauterine Survivability to the New York State Task Force on Life and the Law, *Fetal Extrauterine Survivability* 7 (1988) (hereinafter *Fetal Extrauterine Survivability*). Respirators have been developed that significantly enhance the operation of immature air sacs,[7] but no known technology will accelerate the date at which air sacs begin to form and to link up with the crucial blood vessels. For example, Dr. John Kattwinkel, a member of the American Academy of Pediatric's fetus and newborn committee, has stated:

> At 24 weeks or less, fetal lung development is at a glandular stage and the lung capillaries have not migrated into the airways. You can't force respiration when there is no surface through which to exchange gases. Oxygen simply cannot reach the blood no matter how much air is forced into the lungs by machine.

Pollner, *Abortion: Are medicine and the law on a collision course?*, Medical World News, July 8, 1985, at 73. *See also Fetal Extrauterine Survivability* at 7 ("Clinical experience and anatomic studies suggest that gas exchange is almost never possible before 23 weeks of gestation, but is not uncommon after 26 weeks").[8] There are no medical developments anticipated in the foreseeable future that would bring about adequate fetal lung function prior to 23 to 24 weeks of gestation.

---

[7] See Beddis, Collins, Levy, Godfrey & Silverman, *New technique for servo-control of arterial oxygen tension in preterm infants,* 54 Archives of Disease in Childhood 278-80 (1979).

[8] Air sac development is not the only aspect of lung development that affects viability; it is, however, the factor that sets the outside limit of lung function. For example, the lungs cannot operate without an adequate supply of surfactant, a chemical which prevents the air sacs from collapsing. Inadequate sufactant production is a significant cause of premature infant mortality. The development of surfactant-producing cells cannot be considered an absolute and independent limitation on viability, however, inasmuch as surfactant does not even come into play until the air sacs reach the level of structural sophistication needed to sustain life.

A minimal level of kidney development is also a prerequisite of viability. As observed in *Fetal Extrauterine Survivability*:

> Although the maturational limitations in renal function are an important factor in the morbidity and mortality of [premature] infants with a gestational age less than 26 weeks, renal function is generally not the sole determinant of survival--even down to 24 weeks of gestation. In the earlier 20-24 week gestational period, inadequate kidney development potentially determines fetal survivability.

Fetal Extrauterine Survivability at 6 (footnote omitted).

Amici agree with the overall conclusions expressed in *Fetal Extrauterine Survivability:*

> The increasing ability over the past decade to save progressively younger neonates is primarily due to the ability to support and assist, at an earlier age, the organs already present in the fetus. The developmental biology of the fetus, however, has not changed. After reviewing the developmental biology of several crucial fetal organs, including the brain, the kidneys, and the lungs, the Committee concluded that a point exists before which the fetal organs are too immature to function, even with the assistance of sophisticated medical technology. This point in time is 23-24 week of gestation; *prior to that time, fetal life cannot be maintained outside the womb.*

Id. at 9 (emphasis added).[9]

These conclusions are not contradicted by the studies cited in footnote five of Justice O'Connor's dissenting opinion in *Akron*, 462 U.S. at 457 n. 5, which were characterized as having "demonstrated increasingly earlier fetal viability." One study-- Phillip, Little, Polivy & Lucey, *Neonatal Mortality Risk for the Eighties: The Importance of Birth Weight/Gestational Age Groups*, 68 Pediatrics 122 (1981)-- presents data on premature infant mortality at two medical centers. At one center, data were presented for 523 premature infants treated in an intensive care nursery between 1976 and 1979; of these, five were 25 weeks of gestation or less and only one of the five survived. *Id.* at 125, Table 4.[10] The data from a second regional

---

[9] It should also be noted that even the advance of viability from 24 to 23 weeks is still largely hypothetical. In fact, it is very rare for a fetus delivered before 24 weeks to survive. See, e.g., Milner & Beard, *Limit of Fetal Viability*, 1 Lancet 1079 (1984).

[10] Two of these premature babies weighed between 500 and 749 grams and both died; one baby weighed between 750 and 999 grams and died; and two babies weighed between 1,000 and 1,249 grams and one survived.

medical center showed that infants born alive with a gestational age of less than 25 weeks and weigh between 500 and 1,249 grams had only a 9% survival rate. *Id.* The data in the study do not support the proposition that the point of fetal viability has been moved significantly closer to conception.

The same observations apply to other studies cited in the footnote, and two authors of studies cited there have disassociated themselves from any attempt to use their work as a basis for inferring a shift of the point of viability. For example, Dr. Arthur E. Kopelman, Head of Neonatology at East Carolina School of Medicine-- whose study, *The Smallest Preterm Infants: Reasons for Optimism and New Dilemmas,* 132 American Journal of Diseases of Children 461 (1978) is cited at 462 U.S. at 457 n. 5--subsequently commented:

> I would respond emphatically that my article does not in any way, shape or form support such a contention. Furthermore, I know of no current research which would lead me to believe that a fetus of less than 22 weeks of gestation can be or soon will be able to be sustained outside the uterus. . . .
>
> Below 24 weeks of gestation the fetus' lungs are simply not adequately developed to sustain oxygenation even with ventilator support.

Law, *Rethinking Sex and the Constitution*, 132 U. Pa. L. Rev. 955, 1023-24 n. 245 (1984) (quoting Dr. Kopelman's communication).[11]

---

[11] Similarly, Dr. Leo Stern, Professor and Chairman of Pediatrics at Brown University and the author of *Intensive Care for the Pre-Term Infant*, 26 Danish Med. Bull. 144 (1979), cited at 462 U.S. at 457 n. 5, subsequently wrote:

> It may well be that some of the other references quoted in the footnote have demonstrated "increasingly earlier fetal viability," but that is certainly not what I said in my article. . . . It is highly likely that the lower limit beyond which human gestation is simply incapable of survival has already been virtually reached in its entirety, at least insofar as we intend such survival to be possible without the intervention of some form of artificial extrauterine environment that could be provided by the successful creation of an artificial placenta.

Law, *Rethinking Sex and the Constitution*, 132 U. Pa. L. Rev. 955, 1023-24 n. 245 (1984) (quoting Dr. Stern's communication).

Regarding the development of an artificial placenta, Dr. Stern observed:

> Even if such a procedure could be successfully achieved, not only are its economic costs staggering to imagine but the potential for ever being able to supply the technology in sufficiently large numbers of units to make any kind of impact on the total number of threatened or spontaneously terminated first term gestations would be in practical terms most unlikely.

Id.

In short, the basic scientific observations concerning the outer limit of viability recognized in Roe v. Wade remain accurate.

B. The Organic Capacity for Human Thought Is Absent Until After 28 Weeks Of Gestation

Roe v. Wade established a trimester-based framework for evaluating the interests of a state in protecting fetal life. That framework was supported by reference to the concept of viability. While not mentioned by the Court in *Roe v. Wade,* it is also true that the trimester-based framework corresponds to the chronology of fetal brain development. It is not until sometime after 28 weeks of gestation that the fetal brain has the capacity to carry on the same range of neurological activity as the brain in a full-term newborn.

Fetal brain development is obviously a long and incremental process. Brain cells in the neocortex, the portion of the brain in which the processes we call thought, emotion and consciousness occur, must be sufficiently developed to permit this kind of neurological activity to take place. At about 28 weeks of gestation, brain development is marked by the sudden emergence of dendritic spines in the neocortex. Dendritic spines are essential components in the brain's cellular circuitry.[12]

One study has indicated that neocortical cells possess no dendritic spines as late as 24 to 27 weeks of gestation.[13] It also at that time that large-scale neocortical synaptogenesis (the development of neural connections between brain cells in the neocortex) begins,[14] although limited synaptogenesis may be in as early as 19 to 22 weeks of gestation.[15]

Some primitive motor activities, such as swallowing and spontaneous movement of limbs, begin between eight and thirteen weeks of gestation.[16] However, the thalamocortical connections which are prerequisites for neocortical reception of bodily sensation do not begin to develop until approximately 22 or 23 weeks.[17] In addition,

---

[12] M. Flower, *Neuromaturation and the Moral Status of Human Fetal Life* in Abortion Rights and Fetal Personhood 71, 77 (Doerr & Prescott ed. 1989) (emphasis in original) (forthcoming).

[13] D.P. Purpura, *Morphogensis of Visual Cortex in the Pre-term Infant* in Growth and Development of the Brain, 33, 46 (M.A.B. Brazier ed. 1975) (examining the visual cortex).

[14] *Id.* at 45-46.

[15] Molliver, Kostovic & Van Der Loos, *The development of synapses in cerebral cortex of the human fetus,* 50 Brain Research 403-07 (1973).

[16] Flower, *supra* note 12, at 75.

[17] Kostovic & Goldman-Rakic, *Transient Cholinesterase Staining in the Mediodorsal Nucleus of the Thalamus and its Connections in the Developing Human and Monkey Brain,* 219 Journal of Comparative Neurology 431-47 (1983); Kostovıc & Rakıc, *Development of Prestriate Visual*

regular patterned electroencephalograms (EEGs) with characteristics of an adult EEG appear at approximately 30 weeks.[18] Of course, the fact that the fetus develops the bare biological capacity for crucial neurological processes does not necessarily mean that these neurological processes actually begin to occur in this period. Indeed, the cerebral cortex is relatively nonfunctional even in normal newborns.[19]

The neurobiological data indicate that the fetus lacks the physical capacity for the neurological activities we associate with human thought until sometime after 28 weeks of gestation. In other words, the capacity for the human thought process as we know it cannot exist before that time. *Amici* believe that these neurobiological facts support the chronology of development this Court recognized in *Roe v. Wade*.

CONCLUSION

The parties and the various *amici* in this case may disagree about when a human life begins. Indeed, the signatories of this brief may, as individuals, have different answers to this fundamental question. But such differences are a product of philosophical, moral and religious differences which cannot be resolved by resort to scientific "truth" alone. Those who claim that the Court's decision in *Roe v. Wade* is refuted by scientific law or fact are merely expressing their own value judgments. *Amici* respectfully urge this Court to reject the assertion that *Roe v. Wade* should be overruled on the basis of alleged inconsistency with scientific "truth" and to reaffirm its decision in that case.

Respectfully submitted,

JAY KELLY WRIGHT*
DAVID T. COHEN

ARNOLD & PORTER
1200 New Hampshire Ave., N.W.
Washington, D.C. 20036
(202) 872-6700
Attorneys for Amici Curiae
* Counsel on Record

March 30, 1989
David A. Wollin contributed to the preparation of this brief.

Projections in the Monkey and Human Fetal Cerebrum Revealed by Transient Cholinesterase Staining, 4 Journal of Neuroscience 25-42 (1984).

[18] Flower, *supra* note 12, at 79.

[19] Shewmon, Capron, Warwick & Schulman, *The Use of Amencephalic Infants as Organ Donors: A Critique*, 261 Journal of American Medical Association 1773-81 (1989).

Signers of the Scientists' *Amicus* Brief in *Webster*

Aber, J. Lawrence, Assistant Professor of Psychology, Barnard College of Columbia University

Artavanis-Tsakonas, S., Professor of Biology, Yale University

Axelrod, Julius, Neuroscientist, **Nobel Prize, Medicine, 1970,** National Institute of Mental Health

Ayala, Francisco J., Distinguished Professor of Biological Sciences, University of California

Bejema, Carl Jay, Professor of Biology, Grand Valley State University

Baltimore, David, **Nobel Prize, Physiology or Medicine, 1975,** Director, Whitehead Institute, Professor of Biology, Massachusetts Institute of Technology

Barrett, John N., Professor, University of Miami

Bass, Andrew H., Assistant Professor, Cornell University

Beard, Margaret E., Senior Research Scientist, Nathan Kline Institute

Benacerraf, Baruj, **Nobel Prize, Medicine, 1980,** Chairman, Department of Pathology, Harvard Medical School

Bennett, Michael V.L., Professor and Chairman of Neuroscience, Albert Einstein College of Medicine

Benzer, Seymour, National Medal of Science, 1983, James G. Boswell Professor of Neuroscience, California Institute of Technology

Booker, Ronald, Assistant Professor, Cornell University

Bourden, Douglas M., Professor of Psychiatry and Behavioral Sciences, University of Washington, Director, Regional Primate Research Center

Braine, Lila, Professor, Barnard College of Columbia University

Bullock, Theodore H., Professor of Neurosciences, Emeritus, University of California

Bunge, Mary B., Professor of Anatomy and Neurobiology, Washington University School of Medicine

Bunge, Richard P., Professor of Anatomy and Neurobiology, Washington University School of Medicine

Bush, Guy L., Professor, Department of Zoology, Michigan State University

Cammer, Wendy, Professor of Neurology and Neuroscience, Albert Einstein College of Medicine

Carlson, John R., Assistant Professor of Biology, Yale University

Chambers, Edward L., Professor of Physiology and Biophysics, University of Miami School of Medicine

Cohen, Avis H., Senior Research Associate, Cornell University

Cohen, Lawrence B., Professor, Department of Physiology, Yale University School of Medicine

Crick, Francis, **Nobel Prize, Physiology, 1962**, The Salk Institute

Crill, Wayne E., Professor and Chairman, Department of Physiology and Biophysics, University of Washington

Darnell, James E., Jr., Professor of Molecular Cell Biology, Rockefeller University

Davidson, Eric H., Norman Chandler Professor of Cell Biology, California Institute of Technology

DeRiemer, Susan Λ., Assistant Professor of Biological Sciences, Columbia University

Diamond, Marion, Professor of Anatomy, University of California

Dubach, Mark F., Assistant Professor, University of Washington School of Medicine

Dulbecco, Renato, **Nobel Prize, Physiology or Medicine, 1975**, Distinguished Research Professor and Acting President, The Salk Institute for Biological Studies

Easter, Stephen, Professor of Biology, University of Michigan

Ehrlich, Barbara E., Assistant Professor, Department of Medicine/Cardiology and Physiology, University of Connecticut

Eisen, Judith S., Assistant Professor of Biology, Institute of Neuroscience, University of Oregon

Fernald, Russell D., Institute of Neuroscience, University of Oregon

Fields, Kay Louise, Professor of Neurology and Neuroscience, Albert Einstein College of Medicine

Fischbach, Gerald D., Professor and Chairman, Department of Anatomy and Neurobiology, Washington University School of Medicine

Flower, Michael J., Associate Professor of Biology, Lewis and Clark College

Francoeur, Robert T., Professor of Human Embryology and Medical Ethics, Fairleigh Dickinson University

Gall, Christine, Associate Professor of Anatomy, University of California

Geary, Nori, Associate Professor, Biology Department, Columbia University

Gilbert, Walter, **Nobel Prize, Chemistry, 1980**, Carl M. Loeb University Professor, Harvard University

Goldman-Rakic, Patricia S., Professor of Neuroscience, Yale University School of Medicine

Goldsmith, Timothy H., Professor of Biology and of Ophthamology and Visual Science, Yale University

Goodman, Corey, Professor, Department of Biochemistry, University of California

Gordon-Licky, Barbara, Professor of Psychology, Institute of Neuroscience, University of Oregon

Gordon-Licky, Marvin, Professor of Psychology, Institute of Neuroscience, University of Oregon

Gorlick, Dennis L., Associate Research Scientist, Columbia University

Grinnell, Alan D., Professor of Physiology, UCLA School of Medicine

Hall, Zach W., Professor and Chairman, Department of Physiology, University of California

Hardin, Garrett, Professor Emeritus of Human Ecology, University of California

Harris-Warrick, Ronald M., Associate Professor of Neurobiology and Behavior, Cornell University

Hecht, Norman B., Professor of Biology, Tufts University

Hiatt, Howard H., Professor of Medicine, Harvard Medical School

Hildebrand, John G., Professor of Neurobiology, University of Arizona

Hille, Bertil, Professor of Physiology and Biophysics, University of Washington School of Medicine

Holley, Robert W., **Nobel Prize, Physiology or Medicine, 1968**, Resident Fellow, Molecular Biology, The Salk Institute

Holtzman, Eric, Professor of Biological Sciences, Columbia University

Hopkins, Carl D., Professor, Cornell University

Horowitz, Norman H., Professor of Biology Emeritus, California Institute of Technology

Horvitz, H. Robert, Professor of Biology, Massachusetts Institute of Technology

Howland, Howard C., Professor of Neurobiology and Behavior, Cornell University

Hoy, Ronald R., Professor and Chairman, Section of Neurobiology and Behavior, Cornell University

Hubel, David H., **Nobel Prize, Physiology or Medicine, 1981**, Professor of Neurobiology, Harvard Medical School

Johnson, Bruce R., Senior Research Associate, Section of Neurobiology and Behavior, Cornell University

Kandel, Eric R., National Medal of Science, 1988, Professor, Columbia University College of Physicians and Surgeons, Senior Investigator, Howard Hughes Medical Institute of Molecular Neurobiology and Behavior, Columbia University

Kankel, Douglas R., Associate Professor of Biology, Yale University

Karpf, David B., Associate Professor, Department of Medicine, San Francisco School of Medicine, Associate Investigator in Endocrine Research, VA Medical Center, San Francisco

Keane, Robert W., Assistant Professor, University of Miami School of Medicine

Kelley, Darcy B., Professor, Department of Biological Sciences, Columbia University

Kennedy, Mary B., Associate Professor of Biology, California Institute of Technology

Keshishian, Haig, Assistant Professor, Biology Department, Yale University

Kety, Seymour, Professor Emeritus of Neuroscience in Psychiatry, Harvard Medical School, Senior Scientist, National Institute of Mental Health

Kimble, Daniel P., Professor of Psychology, University of Oregon

Kimmel, Charles B., Professor of Biology, Institute of Neuroscience, University of Oregon

Kleitman, Naomi, Research Associate, Washington University School of Medicine

Konishi, Masakazu, Bing Professor of Behavioral Biology, California Institute of Technology

Korones, Sheldon B., Professor of Pediatrics and of Obstetrics and Gynecology, Director, the Newborn Center, University of Tennessee

Koshland, Daniel E., Jr., Editor of *Science*, Professor of Biochemistry, University of California

Landowne, David, Associate Professor, University of Miami

Lederberg, Joshua, **Nobel Prize, Medicine, 1958**, President, The Rockefeller University

Lerman, Leonard S., Senior Lecturer, Department of Biology, Massachusetts Institute of Technology

Levinthal, Cyrus, Professor of Biology, Columbia University

Levinthal, Francoise, Senior Research Associate, Columbia University

Lewis, Edward B., Thomas Hunt Morgan Professor of Biology, Emeritus, California Institute of Technology

Llinas, Rodolfo R., Chairman and Professor, New York University Medical Center

Lynch, Gary, Professor, Above Scale, Department of Psychobiology, University of California

Macagno, Eduardo R., Professor, Columbia University

Magasanik, Boris, Jacques Monod Professor of Microbiology, Massachusetts Institute of Technology

Magleby, Karl L., Professor of Physiology and Biophysics, University of Miami School of Medicine

Marder, Eve, Associate Professor, Brandeis University

Mayr, Ernst, National Medal of Science, Professor Emeritus, Harvard University

McCulloh, David H., Research Assistant Professor, Department of Physiology and Biophysics, University of Miami School of Medicine

McGlade-McCulloh, Ellen, Research Associate, Department of Physiology and Biophysics, University of Miami School of Medicine

Merrill, Valerie K.L., Postdoctoral Fellow, Brandeis University

Molskness, Theodore A., Research Associate, Oregon Regional Primate Research Center

Moore, Betty C., Research Associate in Biology, University of California

Moore, John A., Professor of Biology, University of California

Muller, Kenneth J., Professor, University of Miami School of Medicine

Neckameyer, Wendi S., Research Associate, Brandeis University

Nirenberg, Marshall, **Nobel Prize, Physiology or Medicine, 1968**, National Institute of Health

O'Day, Peter M., Assistant Professor of Biology and Neuroscience, University of Oregon

Ojeda, Sergio R., Head, Division of Neuroscience, Oregon Regional Primate Research Center

Olson, Everett C., Professor Emeritus of Biology, University of California

Pardue, Mary Lou, Professor of Biology, Massachusetts Institute of Technology

Paton, Martha Constantine, Professor of Biology, Yale University

Perry, Gary W., Research Assistant Professor, Department of Physiology and Biophysics, University of Miami School of Medicine

Podleski, Thomas R., Professor of Neurobiology, Section of Neurobiology and Behavior, Cornell University

Poo, Mu-ming, Professor of Biological Sciences, Columbia University

Purves, Dale, Professor of Neurobiology, Washington University School of Medicine

Rakic, Pasko, Professor of Neuroscience, Yale University School of Medicine

Restifo, Linda L., Postdoctoral Research Associate, Brandeis University

Richardson, Stephen A., Professor Emeritus, Department of Pediatrics, Albert Einstein College of Medicine

Roberts, William M., Assistant Professor, Institute of Neuroscience, University of Oregon

Robins, Diane M., Assistant Professor of Molecular Biology, Columbia University

Role, Lorna W., Assistant Professor, Department of Anatomy and Cell Biology, Columbia University, College of Physicians and Surgeons

Rose, Birgit, Research Associate Professor, Department of Physiology and Biophysics, University of Miami School of Medicine

Rosenberg, Leon E., C.N.H. Long Professor of Human Genetics, Yale University School of Medicine

Rosenblith, Walter A., Institute Professor Emeritus, Massachusetts Institute of Technology

Rothman, Taube P., Research Scientist, Columbia University

Ruibal, Rodolfo, Professor, University of California

Rutila, Joan E., Postdoctoral Fellow, Brandeis University

Ryan, George M.
Professor of Obstetrics and Gynecology, Past President of American College of Obstetrics and Gynecology, University of Tennessee

Sackett, Gene P., Professor, University of Washington

Scharrer, Berta, National Medal of Science, 1983, Distinguished Professor Emerita of Anatomy and Neuroscience, Albert Einstein College of Medicine

Scher, Allen M., Professor, Department of Physiology, University of Washington

Schneiderman, Anne M., Assistant Professor of Neurobiology and Behavior, Cornell University

Schwartz, George J., Professor of Pediatrics, Associate Professor of Physiology/Biophysics, Albert Einstein College of Medicine

Shanklin, Douglas R., Professor of Pathology and of Obstetrics and Gynecology, Chief of Perinatal Pathology and Perinatal Neuropathology, University of Tennessee

Shneour, Elie A., Director, Biosystems Research Institute

Shooter, Eric M., Professor and Former Chairman of Neurobiology, Stanford University School of Medicine

Sibai, Baha M., Professor of Obstetrics and Gynecology, University of Tennessee

Sidman, Richard L., Bullard Professor of Neuropathology, Harvard Medical School

Siegelbaum, Steven A., Associate Professor, Howard Hughes Institute Center for Neurobiology and Behavior, Columbia University

Siekevitz, Philip, Professor, Rockefeller University

Silver, Rae, Professor, Barnard College of Columbia University

Silverman, Ann-Judith, Professor, Department of Anatomy and Cell Biology, Columbia University, College of Physicians and Surgeons

Smith, Orville A., Professor, University of Washington School of Medicine
Director, Regional Primate Research Center

Sperry, Roger, **Nobel Prize, Physiology or Medicine, 1981**, Board of Trustees, Professor of Psychobiology, Emeritus, California Institute of Technology

Spitzer, Adrian, Professor of Pediatrics, Albert Einstein College of Medicine

Spray, David C., Professor of Neuroscience, Albert Einstein College of Medicine

Steiner, Lisa, Professor, Massachusetts Institute of Technology

Steiner, Robert A., Professor, Department of Physiology and Biophysics, University of Washington

Stouffer, Richard L., Scientist, Oregon Regional Primate Research Center

Stuart, Ann E., Professor of Physiology and Ophthamology, University of North Carolina at Chapel Hill

Takahashi, Terry T., Assistant Professor of Biology, Institute of Neuroscience, University of Oregon

Torriani, Annamaria, Professor of Biology, Massachusetts Institute of Technology

Tublitz, Nathan J., Assistant Professor of Biology, University of Oregon

Van Essen, David, Professor and Executive Director for Neurobiology, California Institute of Technology

Van Valen, Leigh M., Professor of Biology, University of Chicago

Vaughan, Herbert G., Jr., Professor of Neuroscience, Neurology and Pediatrics, Director, Rose F. Kennedy Center for Research in Mental Retardation and Human Development, Albert Einstein College of Medicine

Waelsch, Salome G., Professor of Molecular Genetics, Albert Einstein College of Medicine

Wald, George, **Nobel Prize, Physiology or Medicine, 1967**, Professor Emeritus of Biology, Harvard University

Weeks, Janis C., Associate Professor of Biology, Institute of Neuroscience, University of Oregon

Weintraub, Harold M., Member, Fred Hutchinson Cancer Research Center

Weiss, David S., Post Doctoral Fellow, Department of Physiology and Biophysics, University of Miami School of Medicine

Weston, James A., Professor of Biology, Institute of Neuroscience, University of Oregon

White, Kalpana, Associate Professor of Biology, Brandeis University

Williams, Christina L., Associate Professor, Barnard College of Columbia University

Wilson, David L., Dean, College of Arts and Sciences and Professor of Biology, University of Miami

Wilson, Edward O., National Medal of Science, 1977, Baird Professor of Science, Harvard University

Witkin, Joan W., Associate Research Scientist, Department of Anatomy and Cell Biology, Columbia University, College of Physicians and Surgeons

Wold, Barbara J., Associate Professor of Biology, California Institute of Technology

Wyman, Robert J., Professor, Biology Department, Yale University

Zelinski-Wooten, Mary Beth, Research Fellow, Department of Reproductive Biology and Behavior, Oregon Regional Primate Research Center

Zukin, R. Suzanne, Professor of Neuroscience, Albert Einstein College of Medicine

Appendix II

THE CATHOLIC VOTE AND ABORTION

Poll after poll shows that most Catholics are pro-choice. And as voters, they do not follow the bishops—Catholics make up their own minds.

Catholics say abortion should be legal

- A full 82% of US Catholics say abortion should be legal either under certain circumstances or without restrictions.
- This is close to the figure for all Americans: 87%.
- Among Catholics, 39% say a woman should be able to get an abortion if she decides she wants one, no matter what the reason.
- Another 43% say abortion should be legal under certain circumstances, such as when a woman's health is endangered or when a pregnancy results from rape.
- Only 15% of Catholics agree with the bishops' position that abortion should be illegal in all circumstances.

Time/CNN nationwide poll of 1,000 adults, conducted by Yankelovich Partners, September 27-38, 1995, MOE ± 3%; subsample of 500 Catholics, MOE ± 4.5%.

This finding holds true across polls and over time

- 73% of self-described "progressive" Catholics say abortion should be generally available or available with restrictions.
- 43% of self-described "traditional" Catholics say abortion should be generally available for available with restrictions.
- Only 10% of Catholics (and 10% of all Americans) agree with the bishops' position that abortion should be illegal in all cases.

Pew Research Center for People and the Press, June 1996 Religion Survey, May 31-June 9, 1996, and telephone surveys, July 1994-October 1995, of 4,247 adults, MOE ± 3%; subsample of 973 Catholics, MOE ± 4%; subsamples of 212 progressive and 237 traditional Catholics, approximate MOE ± 10%.

- In 1992, 84% of Catholics (and 84% of all Americans) said abortion should be legal in some or all circumstances.
- Only 13% of Catholics agreed with the bishops that abortion should be illegal in all circumstances.

Gallup Survey, for Catholics Speak Out, of 802 Catholics, May 5-7, 1992, MOE ± 4%; and Gallup poll of 1,001 adults nationally, January 16-19, 1992, MOE ± 3% (data provided by the Roper Center, University of Connecticut).

Number of Catholics in the United States: 60 million

Catholics as a portion of total US population: 22%

Catholics as a portion of voters in US House races on Election Day, 1994: 29%

US Catholics who say abortion should be legal in some or all circumstances: 82%

US Catholics who say abortion never can be a morally acceptable choice: 13%

US Catholics saying that a Catholic can vote in good conscience for candidates who support legal abortion: 70%

Importance of abortion in Catholics' voting decisions in the 1994 House races: 9th out of 11 priorities

---

- In 1990, 85% of Catholics (and 90% of all Americans) said abortion should be legal in at least some circumstances.
- 51% of Catholics, like 57% of all Americans, said choices on abortion should be left up to the woman and her doctor.
- Only 12% of Catholics took the bishops' position that abortion should always be illegal.

Wall Street Journal/NBC News poll of 1,555 registered voters nationwide, conducted by Peter Hart and Robert Teeter, July 6-10, 1990, MOE ± 2.6%; subsample of 427 Catholics, MOE ± 5%.

- In 1989, 83% of Catholics (and 83% of all adults) said abortion should be legal, at least in cases of rape/incest or to save the woman's life.
- Among Catholics, only 13% said abortion should always be illegal.

CBS News/New York Times poll of 1,347 adults, September 17-20, 1989, MOE ± 3%; subsample of 341 Catholics, MOE ± 5%.

Catholics believe abortion can be moral

- 64% of Catholics, like 68% of all adults, disapprove or strongly disapprove of the statement that abortion is morally wrong in every case.

US News & World Report survey of 1,000 American adults, conducted by Market Facts' Telenation, designed by Lake Research and Tarrance Group, September 23-24, 1995, MOE ± 3.5%; subsample of 493 Catholics, MOE ± 4.5%.

- Only 13% of Catholics say abortion never can be a morally acceptable choice.
Gallup Survey, for Catholics Speak Out, of 802 Catholics, May 5-7, 1992, MOE ± 4%.

- 69% of Catholics believe a woman who has an abortion for reasons other than to save her life can still be a good Catholic.
ABC/Washington Post poll of 1,530 adults, conducted by Chilton Research Services, September 28-October 1, 1995, MOE ± 3%.

Catholic women have abortions
- Catholic women are as likely as women in the general population to have an abortion.
- Even after standardizing for age and excluding nonwhites and Hispanics (who have higher abortion rates), Catholics are 29 percent more likely than Protestants to have abortions.
Stanley K. Henshaw & Kathryn Kost (Alan Guttmacher Institute), Family Planning Perspectives, vol. 28, no. 4 (July/August 1996), based on an AGI survey of 9,985 women obtaining abortions in 1994-95.

- The same pattern prevailed in 1987-1988.
- When asked why they were having abortions, Catholics were 8% more likely than those of different religious beliefs to say they did not want others to find out about their sexual activity or pregnancy.
Stanley K. Henshaw & Jane Silverman (Alan Guttmacher Institute), Family Planning Perspectives, vol. 20, n. 4 (July/August 1988), based on an AGI survey of 9,480 women obtaining abortions in 1987 and an AGI survey of 1,900 women obtaining abortions in 1987-88.

On abortion as on birth control: Catholics follow their own consciences
- Only 15% of Catholics say a Catholic should always obey official church teachings on such moral issues as birth control and abortion.
- 79% say it is possible for Catholics to make up their own minds on these issues.
- 80% believe it is possible to disagree with the pope on official positions on morality and still be a good Catholic.
Time/CNN nationwide poll of 1,000 adults, conducted by Yankelovich Partners, September 27-28, 1995, MOE ± 3%; subsample of 500 Catholics, MOE ± 4.5%.

- In one recent poll, 82% of Catholics disapproved or strongly disapproved of the statement that using artificial birth control, such as condoms or birth control pills, is morally wrong.
- In another poll, 76% of Catholics disagreed with the statement that using artificial means of birth control is wrong.
82%: US News & World Report survey of 1,000 American adults, conducted by Market Facts' Telenation, designed by Lake Research and Tarrance Group, September 23-24, 1995, MOE ± 3.5%; subsample of 493 Catholics, MOE ± 4.5%. 76%: Time/CNN nationwide poll of 1,000 adults, conducted by Yankelovich Partners, September 27-28, 1995, MOE ± 3%; subsample of 500 Catholics, MOE ± 4.5%.

Catholics go to the polls
- Number of Catholics in the United States: 60 million
- Catholics as a portion of the total US population: 22%

PJ Kenedy & Sons, Official Catholic Directory 1996 (New Providence: NJ: R.R. Bowker, 1996).

- Catholics as a portion of voters who turned out in 1992 on Election Day: 27%
- Catholics, among all voters turning out to vote for US House candidates on Election Day in 1994: 29%

Voter News Service (formerly Voter Research & Surveys) exit polls, 1992 & 1994.

- 77% of US Catholics are registered to vote—just under the 79% registered in the general population.
- 50% of Catholics are among the voters judged "most likely" to vote in the November 1996 elections (on the basis of answers to several questions about voting habits and plans).
- Those "most likely" to vote include 52% of self-described "traditional" Catholics and 47% of self-described "progressive" Catholics.
- This compares to 49% of the general population, 54% of white evangelical Protestants, and 56% of white mainline Protestants.

Pew Research Center for People and the Press, June 1996 Religion Survey, May 31-June 9, 1996, and telephone surveys, July 1994-October 1995, of 4,247 adults, MOE ± 3%; subsample of 973 Catholics; MOE ± 4%; subsamples of 212 progressive and 237 traditional Catholics, approx. MOE ± 10%; voter categories were "most likely," "somewhat likely," or "not likely" to vote.

- Every winning presidential candidate since 1976 has carried a majority or plurality of Catholic voters: 54% for Carter in 1976; a 50% plurality for Reagan in 1980; 54% for Reagan in 1984; 52% for Bush in 1988; and a 44% plurality for Clinton in 1992.

Exit Polls: 1976, CBS; 1980-1988, CBS/New York Times; 1992, Voter News Service.

- In the 1994 House and Senate races, 52% of Catholic voters favored Republicans. In House races alone, 51% voted for Democrats.
- In all House and Senate races, 60% of Protestant voters and 60% of self-identified "religious right" voters favored Republicans.
- Wealthier Catholics were likelier than other Catholics to vote for Republican House and Senate candidates.
- Most Catholics with postgraduate education, or less than a college degree, did not vote Republican. Most of those with a college degree, and no more, did vote Republican.

Roper Center for Public Opinion Research, America at the Polls: 1994.

Abortion is not a litmus test—but Catholics vote prochoice
- Only 9% of US Catholics feel so strongly about abortion that they would not vote

for a political candidate who disagreed with their opinion, regardless of the candidate's stand on other issues.

- This compares to 12% of all Americans.

CBS News/New York Times poll of 1,200 adults, May 31-June 3, 1996, MOE ± 3%; subsample of 294 Catholics, MOE ± 6%.

- Rank of abortion among 11 priorities Catholics considered in deciding how to vote in the 1994 US House races: 9.
- Rank of abortion for all voters: tied for 8-9.
- 39% of Catholics said crime was among their top two priorities, while only 13% cited abortion among the top two.
- Catholics ranked the 11 issues in this order: crime, the economy/jobs, health care, taxes, national issues tied with education, family values/morality, local issues, abortion, campaign finance reform, foreign trade/NAFTA.

Mitofsky International, November 8, 1994, total sample 5,260, including more than 1,000 Catholics.

- The pattern was similar in the 1992 presidential race, with 46% of Catholics saying the economy was among the two most important issues, and only 9% naming abortion.

Voter News Service (then Voter Research & Surveys), exit polls, 1992.

- 66% of Catholics say President Clinton's April 1996 veto of the bill to ban a late-term abortion method will make no difference in their choice between Clinton and Bob Dole in the presidential election—or will make them more likely to vote for Clinton.
- Just after Clinton vetoed the late-term abortion bill, Catholics preferred Clinton over Dole by 58% to 33%.

Los Angeles Times poll of 1,374 adults (1,149 registered voters), April 13-16, 1996, MOE ± 3%; Catholic subsample 418, MOE ± 5%.

- Just after the late-term abortion bill veto, Catholic women, who make up 26% of the female electorate, favored Clinton over Dole by a 61% to 35% margin.

Greenberg/Lake survey of 1089 registered voters, for Emily's List, April 12, 1996.

- 70% of Catholics agree or strongly agree with the statement that Catholics can, in good conscience, vote for political candidates who support legal abortion.

Gallup Survey, for Catholics Speak Out, of 802 Catholics, May 5-7, 1992, MOE ± 4%.

Catholics say religion should not dictate politics
- 77% of Catholics, like 72% of all Americans, say it is not appropriate for religious leaders to urge people to vote for a candidate because of his or her stand on abortion.
- 63% of all Republicans and 73% of all Democrats say it is not appropriate.

CBS News/New York Times poll of 1,200 adults, May 31-June 3, 1996, MOE ± 3%.

- 56% of Catholics (and 55% of non-Catholics) say it is appropriate for religious leaders to take a public position on abortion.
- But 68% of Catholics say it is not appropriate for religious leaders to urge people to vote for or against a candidate because of his or her stand on abortion.
- 65% of non-Catholics say it is not appropriate.

New York Times/CBS News poll of 1,536 adults nationwide, September 18-22, 1995, MOE ± 3%; subsample of 423 Catholics, MOE ± 5%.

- Just before the 1995 papal visit, 73% of US Catholics said that knowing the pope's position on a social or political issue would not influence their position on the issue.
- Only 16% said they would be more likely to support the pope's position.

New York Times/CBS News poll of 1,536 adults nationwide, September 18-22, 1995, MOE ± 3%; subsample of 423 Catholics, MOE ± 5%.

- 79% of Catholics say they are not members or followers of conservative Christian political groups.

Peter D. Hart Research Associates, national survey, for People for the American Way, of 1,252 registered voters, July 19-22, 1995; subsample of 279 Catholics, MOE ± 6.3%.

Appendix III

RELIGIOUS PRO-CHOICE AMERICANS SPEAK OUT

Most religious Americans are pro-choice
For years, religious political extremists have claimed religion opposes abortion. They've said it so often that many people assume it to be true. In fact, this assertion is false. Most religious Americans support a woman's right to choose. They trust women and their families to decide whether and when to have children. They recognize that in a pluralistic society such as ours, the decision regarding abortion must remain with the individual, to be made on the basis of conscience and personal religious principles. They do not want government to impose laws about childbearing based on any one belief about when life begins.

Protestants have longstanding pro-choice positions
Most Protestant denominations in the Untied States have longstanding pro-choice positions. The United Church of Christ has maintained a consistently strong pro-choice stance since 1970. In 1994, the General Convention of the Episcopal Church reaffirmed its position in a resolution expressing "unequivocal opposition to any [legislation] that abridges the right of a woman to reach an informed decision about the termination of pregnancy or that would limit the access of a woman to safe means of acting on her decision." In 1992, the General Assembly of the Presbyterian Church (USA) reaffirmed support for a woman's right to choose; in 1993, the General Assembly voted to affirm the Freedom of Access to Clinic Entrances Act (FACE). At the 1992 General Conference of the United Methodist Church, the principles of *Roe v. Wade* were reaffirmed by an 84 percent majority vote.

Unitarians support abortion rights
The Unitarian Universalist Association affirmed a woman's right to choose in 1963 and has consistently reaffirmed this right at all General Assemblies since then. At the 1993 General Assembly, Unitarian Universalists overwhelmingly adopted a resolution urging members to support federal legislation that would guarantee the basic right to abortion, provide federal funds for abortion to low-income women and military personnel, and protect doctors and clinics providing abortion services from violence and harassment.

Jewish tradition upholds choice
Jewish tradition has long affirmed and protected the life, wellbeing, and health of pregnant women and has upheld the basic right to abortion. The United Synagogue of Conservative Judaism, representing Conservative congregations, in 1993 reaffirmed its resolution opposing any legislative attempts to weaken *Roe v.*

Wade through constitutional amendments. Recent resolutions of the Union of American Hebrew Congregations, representing Reform congregations, uphold an "unwavering commitment to the protection and preservation of the reproductive rights of women" and urge constituents to work toward securing or retaining these rights.